Fast-track Russian

Teach Yourself®

Fast-track Russian

Elisabeth Smith

For UK order enquiries: please contact
Bookpoint Ltd, 130 Milton Park, Abingdon, Oxon OX14 4SB.
Telephone: +44 (0) 1235 827720. Fax: +44 (0) 1235 400454.
Lines are open 09.00–17.00, Monday to Saturday, with a 24-hour
message answering service. Details about our titles and how to
order are available at www.teachyourself.com

For USA order enquiries: please contact
McGraw-Hill Customer Services, PO Box 545, Blacklick,
OH 43004-0545, USA.
Telephone: 1-800-722-4726. Fax: 1-614-755-5645.

For Canada order enquiries: please contact
McGraw-Hill Ryerson Ltd, 300 Water St, Whitby,
Ontario L1N 9B6, Canada.
Telephone: 905 430 5000. Fax: 905 430 5020.

Long renowned as the authoritative source for self-guided learning –
with more than 50 million copies sold worldwide – the teach yourself
series includes over 500 titles in the fields of languages, crafts,
hobbies, business, computing and education.

British Library Cataloguing in Publication Data:
a catalogue record for this title is available from the British Library.

Library of Congress Catalog Card Number: on file.

First published in UK 2000 as *Teach Yourself Instant Russian*
by Hodder Education, part of Hachette UK, 338 Euston Road,
London NW1 3BH.

First published in US 2000 as *Teach Yourself Instant Russian* by
The McGraw-Hill Companies, Inc.

This edition published 2010.

The teach yourself name is a registered trade mark of
Hodder Headline.

Typeset by MPS Limited, A Macmillan Company.

Printed in Great Britain for Hodder Education, an Hachette UK
Company, 338 Euston Road, London NW1 3BH, by CPI Cox &
Wyman, Reading, Berkshire RG1 8EX.

The publisher has used its best endeavours to ensure that the URLs
for external websites referred to in this book are correct and active
at the time of going to press. However, the publisher and the
author have no responsibility for the websites and can make no
guarantee that a site will remain live or that the content will remain
relevant, decent or appropriate.

Hachette UK's policy is to use papers that are natural, renewable
and recyclable products and made from wood grown in sustainable
forests. The logging and manufacturing processes are expected to
conform to the environmental regulations of the country of origin.

Impression number   10 9 8 7 6 5 4 3 2 1
Year   2014 2013 2012 2011 2010

Contents

The author would like to thank Rachel Farmer and Alexandra Borodulina, who acted as language consultants in the preparation of this book.

CREDITS

Read this first

If, like me, you usually skip introductions, don't! Read on! You need to know how **Fast-track Russian** works and why. You'll want to know how you are going to speak Russian in just six weeks.

When I decided to write the **Fast-track** series I first called it *Barebones*, because that's what you want: no frills, no fuss, just the bare bones and go! So in **Fast-track Russian** you'll find:

▶ Only 461 words to say, well … nearly everything.
▶ No tricky grammar – just some useful tips.
▶ No time wasters such as *the pen of my aunt…*
▶ No phrase book phrases for vodka sampling sessions in Siberia.
▶ No need to be perfect. Mistakes won't spoil your success.

I've put some 30 years of teaching experience into this course. I know how people learn. I also know how long they are motivated by a new project before the boredom sets in (a few weeks). And I am well aware how little time they can spare to study each day (just over ½ hour). That's why you'll complete **Fast-track Russian** in six weeks and get away with 45 minutes a day.

Of course there is some learning to do, but I have tried to make it as much fun as possible. You'll meet Tom and Kate Walker on holiday in Russia. They do the kind of things you need to know about: shopping, eating out and getting about. They chat to the locals, ask a lot of questions and even understand the answers – most of the time! As you will note, Tom and Kate speak **Fast-track Russian** all the time, even to each other. What paragons of virtue!

To get the most out of this course, there are only three things you really should do:

- Follow the **Day-by-day** guide as suggested. Please don't skip bits and short-change your success. Everything is there for a reason.
- If you are a complete beginner and have only bought the book, treat yourself to the recording as well. It will help you to speak faster and with confidence.
- Don't skip the next page (**How this book works**). It's essential for your success.

When you have filled in your **Certificate** at the end of the book and can speak **Fast-track Russian**, I would like to hear from you. Why not visit my website www.elisabeth-smith.co.uk, e-mail me at elisabeth.smith@hodder.co.uk, or write to me care of Hodder Education, 338 Euston Road, London, NW1 3BH?

Elisabeth Smith

How this book works

Fast-track Russian has been structured for your rapid success. This is how it works:

Day-by-day guide Stick to it. If you miss a day, add one.

Dialogues Follow Tom and Kate through Russia. The English is in 'Russian-speak' to get you tuned in. 'Russian-speak' is English imitating the expressions and word order of Russian: We have a house big without telephone. You'll soon get a feel for the language.

New words Don't fight them, don't skip them – learn them! The **Flash cards** and the recording will help you. Get your friends or family to test you. Or take the **Flash cards** with you when you are out and about.

Good news grammar After you read it you can forget half and still succeed! That's why it's good news.

Flash words and flash sentences Read about these building blocks in the **Flash card** section. Then use them! They'll reduce learning time by 50%.

Learn by heart Obligatory! Memorizing puts you on the fast track to speaking in full sentences. When you know all six pieces you'll be able to speak in Russian for six minutes without drawing breath.

Let's speak Russian You will be doing the talking – in Russian.

Let's speak more Russian – fast and fluently Optional extras for more speaking practice without pausing and stumbling.

Spot the keys Listen to rapid Russian and make sense of it. Find the key words among a seemingly unintelligible string of sentences and get the gist of what's being said – an essential skill.

Say it simply Learn how to use plain, **Fast-track Russian** to say what you want to say. Don't be shy.

Test your progress Mark your own test and be amazed by the result.

Answers This is where you'll find the answers to the exercises.

◄◙ This icon asks you to switch on the recording.

Pronunciation If you don't know about it and don't have the recording go straight to **Week 1 Pronunciation**. You need to know about pronunciation before you can start Week 1.

Progress chart Enter your score each week and monitor your progress. Are you going for very good or outstanding?

Dictionary Forgotten one of the **fast-track** words? Look it up in the dictionary.

Certificate It's on the last page. In six weeks it will have your name on it.

Progress chart

At the end of each week record your test score on the progress chart below.

At the end of the course throw out your worst result – anybody can have a bad week – and add up your five best weekly scores. Divide the total by five to get your average score and overall course result. Write your result – *outstanding*, *excellent*, *very good* or *good* – on your **Certificate** at the end of the book.

PROGRESS CHART

90–100%							outstanding
80–89%							excellent
70–79%							very good
60–69%							good
Weeks	1	2	3	4	5	6	

Total of five best weeks =

divided by five =

Your final result _____ %

Only got a minute?

If you only have one minute spare, have a look at the following.

Would you like to meet and greet someone?

To say *hello* in Russian you'd say **zdrastvooiytee**.

To find out how someone is you'd ask **kak deela**.

The answer to **kak deela**, *how are you?*, is usually **kharasho** – that's *good* or *well*.

Going home and want to say *goodbye*? Say **da sveedaneeya**.

And if you get stuck you could always ask **Vy gavareetee po-angleeskee?** *Do you speak English?*

5 Only got five minutes?

Here's what you can learn in five minutes.

Would you like to meet and greet someone?

To say *hello* in Russian you'd say **zdrastvooiytee**.

Good morning is **dobraye ootra** and during the day you say **dobriiy dyen** – that's *good day*.

To find out how someone is you'd ask **kak deela**.

The answer to **kak deela**, *how are you?*, is usually **kharasho** – that's good or well.

Thank you, *very well* is **spaseeba, ocheen' kharasho**.

Going home and want to say *goodbye*? Say

da sveedaneeya.

And if you get stuck you could always ask

Vy gavareetee po-angleeskee? *Do you speak English?*

10 Only got ten minutes?

Here's what you can learn in ten minutes.

Would you like to meet and greet someone and find out where things are and ask for directions?

To say *hello* in Russian you'd say **zdrastvooiytee**.

Good morning is **dobraye ootra** and during the day you say **dobriiy dyen'** – that's *good day*. *Good evening* is **dobriiy vyecheer**.

To find out how someone is you'd ask **kak deela**.

The answer to **kak deela**, *how are you?*, is usually **kharasho** – that's *good* or *well*.

Thank you, very well is **spaseeba, ocheen' kharasho**.

Going home and want to say *goodbye*? Say **da sveedaneeya**.

Where is...? is **gdye?**

Where's a bus? would be **gdye aftoboos**?

A *supermarket* is **soopeermarkeet**, so *where's the supermarket?* is **gdye soopeermarkeet**?

If you don't know a particular word use body language to explain what you are looking for.

When you want to find your way it will help you to know *left*, *right* and *straight ahead*.

On the left is **nalyeva**, *on the right* is **naprava** and *straight on* is **pryama**.

If you want to know if something is far you'd ask **Eta daleeko**? *Is it far?*

And if you get stuck you could always ask **Vy gavaritee po-angleeskee**? *Do you speak English?*

1

Week one

DAY-BY-DAY GUIDE

Study for 45 minutes a day – or a little longer if you can!

DAY ZERO

▶ Open the book and read **Read this first**.
▶ Now read **How this book works**.

DAY ONE

▶ Read **In the aeroplane**.
▶ Listen to/Read **F samalyotee**.
▶ Listen to/Read the **New words**, then learn some of them.

DAY TWO

▶ Repeat **F samalyotee** and the **New words**.
▶ Listen to/Read **Pronunciation**.
▶ Learn more **New words**.

DAY THREE

▶ Learn all the **New words** until you know them well.
▶ Use the **Flash words** to help you.
▶ Read and learn the **Good news grammar**.

DAY FOUR

▶ Cut out and learn the **Flash sentences**.
▶ Listen to/Read **Learn by heart**.

DAY FIVE

▶ Listen to/Read **Let's speak Russian**.
▶ Revise! Tomorrow you'll be testing your progress.

DAY SIX

▶ Listen to/Read **Let's speak more Russian** (optional).
▶ Listen to/Read **Let's speak Russian – fast and fluently** (optional).
▶ Translate **Test your progress**.

DAY SEVEN

This is your day off!

IN THE AEROPLANE

Tom and Kate Walker are on their way to Russia. They are boarding flight SU 254 to Yalta via Moscow and squeeze past Yuriy Zhivago who is sitting in their row. Don't forget that the English is in 'Russian-speak' to help you get used to the way the language works.

Tom Excuse me, please, by us (we have) seats 9a and 9b.

Yuriy Yes?... little minute (just a moment), please.

Tom Hello. We – Tom and Kate Walker.

Yuriy Hello. Me they call (I am called) Zhivago.

Tom Dr Zhivago?

Yuriy No, unfortunately. I – Yuriy Zhivago.

Tom We are going to Yalta. You also?

Yuriy No, I am going to Moscow. But I from Novgorod.

Tom Novgorod very beautiful town. I was there in May, on business.

Yuriy Who you? (What do you do?)

Tom I programmer. Computers. I work at Unilever.

Yuriy And you, Mrs Walker? Who you? Where do you work?

Kate I worked in travel agency. Now I work in Rover. The work there better.

Yuriy You from London?

Kate No, we from Manchester. We were three years in London and a year in New York. Now we in Birmingham.

Yuriy I worked in the university. Now I work in bank.

Kate Work in bank good?

Yuriy Work boring. But money (of money) more. By me (I have) big flat, Mercedes, wife, son and daughter. My wife from America. By her (she has) parents in Los Angeles and girlfriend in Florida. She always rings to them. It (is) costs expensive.

Kate We now in holiday (on holiday). You also?

Yuriy No, unfortunately. By me (I have) in August holiday. We are going to Greece. By us (we have) there house... summer home – without telephone. And we go there without mobile phone!

14

F SAMALYOTEE

The letters in bold indicate the stress the syllable in which they appear.
The first word of the dialogue below is *excuse me* – 'eez-vee-**nee**-tee'.
You would stress the penultimate syllable. When you find a bold *o*
you pronounce it like the *o* in *bore*. If it isn't bold it's like the *a* in *sofa*.

Tom and Kate Walker are on their way to Russia. They are
boarding flight SU 254 to Yalta via Moscow and squeeze past
Yuriy Zhivago who is sitting in their row.

CD1, TR 2

Tom	Eezveen**ee**tee, pazh**a**loosta, oo nas meest**a** 9a ee 9b.
Yuriy	D**a**?... meen**oo**tachkoo, pazh**a**loosta.
Tom	Zdr**a**stvooiytee. Mi – Tom ee Kate Walker.
Yuriy	Zdr**a**stvooiytee. Meen**ya** zav**oo**t Zhiv**a**ga.
Tom	D**o**ktar Zhiv**a**ga?
Yuriy	Nyet, k sazhil**ye**neeyu. Ya –**Yu**riy Zhiv**a**ga.
Tom	Mi **ye**deem v **Ya**ltoo. Vi t**o**zhe?
Yuriy	Nyet. Ya **ye**doo v Maskv**oo**. No ya eez N**o**vgarada.
Tom	N**o**vgarat **o**cheen' kras**ee**viiy g**o**rat. Ya tam bil v m**a**ee, pa b**ee**znisoo.
Yuriy	Kto vi?
Tom	Ya pragram**ee**st. Kamp'**yu**tiri. Ya rab**o**tayu v Oonee**lee**veerye.
Yuriy	A vi, m**ee**sees Walker? Kto vi? Gdee vi rab**o**taeetee?
Kate	Ya rab**o**tala v toorag**ye**ntstvee. Seech**ya**s ya rab**o**tayu v R**o**veerye. Rab**o**ta tam l**oo**chshe.
Yuriy	Vi eez L**o**ndana?
Kate	Nyet. Mi eez Manch**ye**s'teera. Mi b**i**lee tree g**o**da v L**o**ndanee ee got v Nyu Y**o**rkee. Seech**ya**s mi v Beermeeng**ye**mee.
Yuriy	Ya rab**o**tal v oonee**v**eerseet**ye**tee. Seech**ya**s ya rab**o**tayu v b**a**nkee.
Kate	Rab**o**ta v b**a**nkee khar**o**shaya?
Yuriy	Rab**o**ta sk**oo**chnaya. No d**ye**neek b**o**l'shi. Oo meen**ya** bal'sh**a**ya kvart**ee**ra, Meers**ee**des, zhin**a**, sin ee doch. M**a**ya zhin**a** eez Am**ye**reekee. Oo nee**yo** rad**ee**teeli v Los **A**nzhileesee ee padr**oo**ga v Flar**ee**dee. An**a** vseegd**a** zvan**ee**t eem. **E**ta st**o**eet d**o**raga.
Kate	Mi seech**ya**s v **o**tpooskee. Vi t**o**zhe?
Yuriy	Nyet, k sazhil**ye**neeyu. Oo meen**ya** v **a**vgoostee **o**tpoosk. Mi **ye**deem v Gr**ye**tsiyu. Oo nas tam dom... d**a**chya – bees teel**ee**f**o**na. Mi **ye**deem tood**a** bees s**o**tavava!

NEW WORDS

◄ CD1, TR 3

Learning words the traditional way can be boring. If you enjoy the **Flash cards** why not make your own for the rest of the words? Always say the words out loud. It's the fast track to speaking!

v, va, f *in, to, at*
samal**yot**(ee) *aeroplane*
eezvee**nee**tee *excuse me*
pazh**a**loosta *please*
oo nas *by us (we have)*
m**ee**sta *places, seats*
a... b a... b (pronounced ah... *bay*)
ee *and*
da *yes*
meen**oo**tachkoo *little minute*
zdr**a**stvooiytee *hello*
mi *we*
meen**ya** zav**oo**t *they call me (I am called)*
nyet *no*
k sazhil**ye**neeyu *unfortunately*
ya *I*
yedeem *we go (travel)*
yedoo *I go (travel)*
vi *you (polite)*
t**o**zhe *also*
no *but*
eez, ees *from*
ocheen' *very*
kras**ee**viy *beautiful*
g**o**rad, g**o**rat *town*
tam *there*
bil *was*

bilee *were*
v m**a**ee *in May*
dly**a** *for*
pa b**ee**znisoo on *business*
kto *who*
rab**o**tayu *I work*
rab**o**taeetee *you work*
pragram**ee**st *computer programmer*
kamp'**yu**tir/kamp'**yu**tiri *computer*
gdye *where*
rab**o**tala *I, she worked*
rab**o**tal *I, he worked*
v toorag**ye**ntstvee *in a/the travel agency*
seech**ya**s *now*
rab**o**ta *work, job*
l**oo**chshe *better*
tree *three*
g**o**da/got *year*
v ooneeveerseet**ye**tee *at a/ the university*
bank/v b**a**nkee *bank/in, at bank*
khar**o**chaya *good*
sk**oo**chnaya *boring*
d**ye**neek *money*
bol'shi *more*

oo meen**ya** *I have*
bal'sh**aya** *big*
kvart**ee**r**a** *flat*
m**aya**, moiy *my*
zhin**a** *wife*
sin *son*
doch *daughter*
oo nee**yo** *she has*
rad**ee**teelee *parents*
padr**oo**g**a** *girlfriend*
an**a** *she*
vseegd**a** *always*
zvan**ee**t *rings, phones*

eem *to them*
et**a** *it is*
st**o**eet *costs*
dor**a**g**a** *expensive*
v **o**tpooskee *on holiday*
v **a**vgoos'tee *in August*
tam *there*
dom *house*
d**a**chya *summer house*
bees teelef**o**n**a** *without telephone*
s**o**taviy (teelef**o**n) *mobile telephone*

TOTAL NEW WORDS: 75…
only 306 words to go!

SOME EASY EXTRAS

MYESEETSI (MONTHS)

yanv**a**r', feevr**a**l', mart, apr**ye**l', m**a**iy, ee**yu**n', ee**yu**l', **a**vgoost,
seent**ya**br', akt**ya**br', n**a**yabr', d**ee**kabr'

TSIFRI (NUMERALS)

ad**ee**n 1
dva 2
tree 3
cheetiree 4
pyat' 5

sh**e**s't' 6
syem' 7
v**o**seem' 8
d**ye**veet' 9
d**ye**seet' 10

MORE GREETINGS

d**o**braye **oo**tra *good morning* d**o**briiy dyen' *good day, good afternoon*
d**o**briiy **vye**cheer *good evening* d**a** sveed**a**neeya *goodbye*

PRONUNCIATION

◀) CD1, TR 4

The Russian language is beautiful, so drop all inhibitions and try to speak Russian rather than English with the words changed. If Russian pronunciation is new to you, please buy the recording and listen to the real thing.

As you can see, all the words **in Fast-track Russian** have been transliterated into phonetic language. That makes it much easier, especially if you are in a hurry. You don't have to learn the Cyrillic alphabet first but can start speaking straight away.

The guide to vowels and consonants will get you started. Sometimes it takes a lot of English letters – for example **shsh** – to produce the sound of one Russian letter, but you'll soon pick it up.

And don't worry if you don't get it exactly right. Near enough is good enough.

VOWELS

Say the sound out loud and then the Russian example out loud.

a	like *a* in *father*	bal'sh**a**ya
e	like *e* in *let*	**e**ta
ee	like *ee* in *feet*	eezvee**nee**tee
i	like *i* in *still*	m**i**
iy	like *y* in *boy*	kras**ee**viy
o	like *o* in *bore*	L**o**ndan
oo	like *oo* in *shoot*	l**oo**chshee

Y PLUS VOWEL

ya	like *ya* in *yard*	ya
ye	like *ye* in *yet*	nyet
yo	like *yo* in *yonder*	oo nee**yo**
yu	like *u* in *universal*	ya rab**o**tayu

CONSONANTS

g	is always pronounced as a 'hard' **g**, as in *goat*	
r	is rolled (as in Italian)	
v	like *v* in *vase*	
zh	like *s* in *pleasure*	to**zhe**
kh	like *ch* in *loch*	khar**o**shaya
ts	like *ts* in *quits*	tsar
sh	like *sh* in *shout*	shes't'
shsh	like *sh* in *posh ship*	eeshsh**yo**
l', t'		sk**o**l'ka
iy	like *y* in *toy*	m**a**iy

When you see a ' after a letter try to slip in a very soft **y**.

ACCENT

The letter in **bold** tells you to stress the syllable in which it appears. Example: Mask**voo**, rab**o**tayu. The stress is especially important when you come across the vowel **o**. If it is stressed, it is pronounced like the *o* in *bore*; if it is not stressed, it is pronounced like the *a* in *sofa*.

When you go to Russia you'll want to know a little of the Cyrillic script, too. So, as an introduction, here's the Russian alphabet. And later in the course there'll also be a few useful flash words in 'real' Russian script, to help you on your way.

А Б В Г Д Е Ё Ж З И Й К Л М Н О П Р
а б в г д е ё ж з и й к л м н о п р
С Т У Ф Х Ц Ч Ш Щ Ъ Ы Ь Э Ю Я
с т у ф х ц ч ш щ ъ ы ь э ю я

GOOD NEWS GRAMMAR

🔊 CD1, TR 5

This is the good news part of each week. Remember I promised *no ghastly grammar*! I simply explain the differences between Russian and English. This will help you to speak **fast-track** Russian.

1 WORDS FOR 'THE' AND 'A'

There aren't any! So **bank** in Russian means either *a bank* or *the bank* and the plural **bankee** means either *some banks* or *the banks*.

2 THE RUSSIAN WORDS FOR 'AM', 'ARE', 'IS'

There aren't any! So all you need to say in Russian is:

> *I computer programmer* = **ya** **pragrameest**

3 THE RUSSIAN WORDS FOR 'HAVE', 'HAS'

There aren't any! Russian uses a different sort of phrase and says, literally, *by me (there is)* = **Oo meenya.**

Example: *I have a flat.* = **Oo meenya kvarteera.**

Here is the complete list. Spend ten minutes on it until you know it with your eyes closed.

oo meen**ya**	*I have*
oo vas	*you have*
oo neev**o**, oo nee**yo**	*he has, she has*
oo nas	*we have*
oo neekh	*they have*

4 SAYING 'YOU'

Russian has two words for you. If you know one person well, or are speaking to a child, use ti; if you are being polite and formal to one person use vi or if you are speaking to more than one person, also use vi. In **Fast-track Russian** you only use vi.

5 DOING THINGS

Did you notice that when you say *I, we* or *you* in Russian the ending of the verb changes? Here are the verbs you came across in the dialogue. Have another look at them. They are not for learning. You have done that already.

rabotat' to work	
ya rab**o**tayu	*I work*
mi rab**o**taeem	*we work*
vi rab**o**taeetee	*you work*

yekhat' to travel	
ya **ye**doo	*I travel*
mi **ye**deem	*we travel*
vi **ye**deetee	*you travel*

6 V: *IN, AT, TO*

As you saw in the **New words** the Russian letter v (va)/f can mean *in, at, to* and sometimes even *on,* as in *on holiday* – v **otpooskee**. That's the easy bit. Unfortunately, after a v the ending of the following word changes. So **Maskva** becomes **Maskvoo** (*to Moscow*) and **bank** becomes **bankye** (*at the bank*). But don't worry about it. This is just for knowing, not for learning! You'll pick it up as you go along.

7 ASKING QUESTIONS

'Vi tozhe'. *You, too.* 'Vi tozhe?' *You, too?* You simply use your voice to turn a statement into a question. Easy!

LEARN BY HEART

Don't be tempted to skip this exercise because it reminds you of school... If you want to speak, not stumble, saying a few lines by heart does the trick!

Learn 'Meenya zavoot' by heart after you have filled in the gaps with your personal, or any, information.

Example: Meenya zavoot Colin Bell.
　　　　　 Ya eez Londana.

When you know the seven lines by heart, go over them again until you can say them out loud fluently and fairly fast. Can you beat 40 seconds?

Meenya zavoot

Meenya zavoot .... (NAME)
Ya eez .... (PLACE)
Ya rabotayu v bankee ....
Oo meenya bal'shaya kvarteera. Ana doroga stoeet.
V martee ya bil/bila v .... (PLACE)
F seenteebrye mi yedeem v .... (PLACE)
Vi tozhe?

LET'S SPEAK RUSSIAN

🔊 CD1, TR 7

I shall give you ten English sentences and you'll put them into Russian. Always speak out loud. After each one check the answer at the bottom of the page. Tick it if you got it right. If you have the recording, listen to check the answers to **Let's speak Russian**.

1 I am called Tom Walker.
2 Are you from London?
3 Yes, I am from London.
4 I have a girlfriend in Florida.
5 We are going to Moscow.
6 Do you have a Mercedes?
7 No, unfortunately (not).
8 We have a house in Novgorod.
9 There is more money in the bank.
10 Is the job boring?

Well, how many did you get right? If you are not happy, do it again! Now here are some questions in Russian and you are going to answer in Russian. Answer the next five questions with da and ya.

11 Vi eez Manchyes'teera?
12 Oo vas dom v Londanee?
13 Vi yedeetee v Maskvoo?
14 Vi rabotaeetee bees komp'yutera?
15 Vi bilee v Breestolee pa beeznisoo?

And now answer the next five questions with da and ya, mi or oo nas.

16 Vi yedeetee v Novgarat?
17 Oo vas meesta 9a ee 9b?
18 Oo vas otpoosk v apryelee?
19 Vi bilee tree goda v Londanee?
20 Oo vas seechyas bol'shi dyeneek?

Answers

1 *Meenya zavoot Tom Walker.*
2 *Vi eez Londana?*
3 *Da, ya eez Londana.*
4 *Oo meenya padrooga v Flareedee.*
5 *Mi yedeem v Maskvoo.*
6 *Oo vas Meerseedes?*
7 *Nyet, k sazhilyeneeyu.*
8 *Oo nas dom v Novgaradee.*
9 *V bankee bol'shi dyeneek.*
10 *Rabota skoochnaya?*
11 *Da, ya eez Manchyes'teera.*
12 *Da, oo meenya dom v Londanee.*

13 *Da, ya yedoo v Maskvoo.*
14 *Da, ya rabotayu bees komp'yutera.*
15 *Da, ya bil/bila v Breestolee pa beeznisoo.*
16 *Da, ya yedoo v Novgarat.*
17 *Da, oo nas meesta 9a ee 9b.*
18 *Da, oo nas otpoosk v apryelee.*
19 *Da, mi bilee tree goda v Londanee.*
20 *Da, oo nas seechyas bol'shi dyeneek.*

Well, what was your score? If you ticked all of them give yourself a big pat on the back.

LET'S SPEAK MORE RUSSIAN

◀) **CD1, TR 8**

Here are some optional exercises. They may stretch the 45 minutes a day by 15 minutes. But the extra practice will be worth it.

And always remember: near enough is good enough!

IN YOUR OWN WORDS

This exercise will teach you to express yourself freely. Use only the words you have learned so far.

Tell me in your own words that...

1 you are from Manchester
2 unfortunately your work is boring
3 you have a son and daughter
4 you work in a university
5 you have a house in Birmingham
6 you are going to Moscow
7 you have a friend in London
8 Yalta is a very beautiful town
9 you are on holiday
10 a big flat in New York is very expensive

···

Answers

1 *Ya eez Manchyes'tyera.*
2 *K sazhilyeneeyu rabota skoochnaya.*
3 *Oo myenya sin ee doch.*
4 *Ya rabotayu v ooneevyeerseetyetee.*
5 *Oo meenya dom v Beermeengyemee.*
6 *Ya yedoo v Maskvoo.*
7 *Oo meenya padrooga v Londanee.*
8 *Yalta ocheen' kraseeviiy gorat.*
9 *Oo meenya otpoosk.*
10 *Bal'shaya kvarteera v Nyu Yorke stoeet ocheen' doraga.*

———————————————————

LET'S SPEAK RUSSIAN – FAST AND FLUENTLY

◀) **CD1, TR 9**

No more stuttering and stumbling! Get out the stopwatch and time yourself with this fluency practice. Some of the English is in 'Russian-speak' to help you.

Translate each section and check if it is correct. Then cover up the answers and say the three or four sentences fast! Try to say each group of sentences in less than 30 seconds.

Good morning. I am going to Moscow. You too?
No, I work in New York – in a bank. Now I am going to Yalta on business.
My wife is from Novgorod.
I have in September holiday – without telephone.

Dobraye ootra. Ya **ye**doo v Maskv**oo**. Vi t**o**zhe?
Nyet, ya rab**o**tayu v Nyu Y**o**rke – v b**a**nkee. Seech**a**s ya **ye**doo v **Ya**ltoo pa b**ee**znis**oo**.
May**a** zhin**a** eez N**o**vgar**a**da.
Oo meen**ya** v seent**ee**br**ye o**tpoosk – bees teel**ee**f**o**na.

Hello. Who you?
Me they call John. I have a girlfriend, Tanya. She programmer.
In bank in Moscow.
I work in university. The work there very good.

Zdrastv**oo**iytee. Kto vi?
Meen**ya** zav**oo**t John. Oo meen**ya** padr**oo**ga, T**a**nya. An**a** pragram**ee**st. V b**a**nkee v Maskv**ye**.
Ya rab**o**tayu v oon**ee**veerseet**ye**tee. Rab**o**ta tam khar**o**shaya.

I have flat in Moscow. Costs very expensive.
We were two years in Moscow. Moscow very beautiful town.
Now we in London.
Excuse me, little minute (just a moment), please. My wife rings.

Oo meen**ya** kvart**ee**ra v Maskv**ye**. St**o**eet **o**cheen' d**o**raga.
Mi b**i**lee dva goda v Maskv**ye**. M**a**skva **o**cheen' kras**ee**viiy g**o**rat.
Seech**a**s mi v L**o**ndanee.
Eezveen**ee**tee, meen**oo**tachkoo, pazh**a**loosta. May**a** zhin**a** zvan**ee**t.

TEST YOUR PROGRESS

This is your only written exercise. You'll be amazed at how easy it is! Translate the 20 sentences without looking at the previous pages. The bits in brackets help you with the difference between English and Russian.

(Please note: write the words straight: don't alternate bold type and light to show where the word is stressed. It would take you forever!)

1 They call me (I am called) Frank Lukas.
2 Hello, we (are) Viktor and Olga.
3 I (am) also from Omsk.
4 In October I was in Moscow.
5 We were three years in America.
6 London is very expensive.
7 Excuse me, please. Where (do) you work?
8 Are you working in Manchester?
9 (Are) you Viktor Izmailov from Tomsk?
10 (The) flat in Novgorod is very big.
11 Little minute (just a moment), please, by me (I have) more money.
12 There there is (a) telephone? No, unfortunately not.
13 I (am) in Yalta without (my) son.
14 (Is) (the) company big?
15 (Is) (a) Mercedes expensive?
16 In April London (is) very beautiful.
17 By him (he has) in (the) travel agency (a) girlfriend.
18 Unfortunately (the) work (is) very boring.
19 (The) job is very good, but (a) holiday is better.
20 My daughter telephones always.

When you have finished look up the answers in the **Answers** section and mark your work. Then enter your result on the **Progress chart** at the front of the book. If your score is higher than 80% you'll have done very well indeed!

2

Week two

DAY-BY-DAY GUIDE

Forty-five minutes a day – but a little extra will step up your progress!

DAY ONE

▶ Read In **Saint Petersburg.**
▶ Listen to/Read **f Sankt-Peeteerboorgee.**
▶ Listen to/Read the **New words.** Learn 20 easy ones.

DAY TWO

▶ Repeat **f Sankt-Peeteerboorgee** and the **New words.**
▶ Go over **Pronunciation.**
▶ Learn the harder **New words.**
▶ Use the **Flash words** to help you.

DAY THREE

▶ Learn all the **New words** until you know them well.
▶ Read and learn the **Good news grammar.**

DAY FOUR

▶ Cut out and learn the **Flash sentences.**
▶ Listen to/Read **Learn by heart.**

DAY FIVE

▶ Listen to/Read **Let's speak Russian.**
▶ Go over **Learn by heart.**

DAY SIX

▶ Listen to/Read **Let's speak more Russian** (optional).
▶ Listen to/Read **Let's speak Russian – fast and fluently** (optional).
▶ Translate **Test your progress.**

DAY SEVEN

This is a study-free day!

IN SAINT PETERSBURG

In Saint Petersburg Tom and Kate are checking in to a hotel. They speak to Olga, the receptionist at the service desk and later to Ivan, the waiter.

Kate	Good day. By you (do you have) room for two, for one night? Costs not too expensive?
Olga	Yes, by us (we have) room with a bath and shower… but shower it is necessary to repair, it does not work.
Tom	Where is room?
Olga	On tenth floor.
Kate	How much does it cost?
Olga	Only 500 roubles per person, but credit cards we do not accept! Breakfast from eight o'clock to nine.
Tom	Well… we want room. But is it possible to have breakfast at 7.45? By us (we have) excursion tomorrow at 8.15.
Kate	And I have question. Where is it possible to drink coffee or tea? Where here café?
Olga	Café from here is near, to the left, then to the right 30 metres, then straight on.
(In the café…)	
Ivan	I am listening you (What can I get you?).
Kate	For us coffee without sugar and tea with milk.
Ivan	Is it all? By us (we have) sandwiches with cheese and with ham.
Tom	One sandwich with cheese and one with ham, please.
Tom	Cheese terrible.
Kate	But ham good.
Tom	Table too small.
Kate	But toilets very clean.
Tom	My tea cold.
Kate	But waiter very beautiful (handsome).
Tom	Bill, please.
Ivan	Fifty roubles.

F SANKT-PEETEERBOORGEE

In Saint Petersburg Tom and Kate are checking in to a hotel. They speak to Olga, the receptionist at the service desk and later to Ivan, the waiter.

Kate Dobriiy dyen'. Oo vas yes't' nomeer na dvaeekh, na adnoo noch? Stoeet nee sleeshkam doraga?

Olga Da, oo nas nomeer s vanay ee s dooshim… a doosh nada atreemanteeravat', on nye rabotaeet.

Tom Gdye nomeer?

Olga Na desyatam itazhe.

Kate Skol'ka stoeet?

Olga Tol'ka peet'sot rooblyeiy na cheelavyeka, no kreedeetniee kartachkee mi nye preeneemaeem! Zaftrak s vas'mee cheesof da deeveeatee.

Tom Noo… mi khateem nomeer. A mozhna zaftrakat' f syem' sorak pyat'? Oo nas ikskoorseeya zaftra v voseem' peetnatsat.

Kate Ee o meenya vapros. Gdye mozhna peet' kofee eelee chyaiy? Gdye z'dyes' kafe?

Olga Kafe atsyuda bleeska, nalyeva, patom naprava treetsat myetraf, patom pryama.

(In the café…)

Ivan Slooshayu vas.

Kate Nam kofee bees sakhara ee chyaiy s malakom.

Ivan Eta fsyo? Oo nas bootibrodi s siram ee s veetcheenoiy.

Tom Adeen bootibrot s siram ee adeen s veetcheenoiy, pazhaloosta.

Tom Sir oozhasniiy.

Kate A veetcheena kharoshaya.

Tom Stol sleeshkam maleenkeeiy.

Kate A tooalyeti ocheen' cheestiee.

Tom Moiy chyaiy khalodniy.

Kate A afeetsiant kraseeviiy.

Tom Shshyot, pazhaloosta.

Ivan Peedeesyat rooblyiey.

NEW WORDS

dobriiy dyen' *good day*
yes't' *there is/is there*
nomeer na dvaeekh *room for two (i.e. double room)*
na *for, on*
na adnoo noch *for one night*
nye *not*
sleeshkam *too (as in too much)*
s, z *with, from*
s vanaiy *with a bathroom*
doosh (z dooshim) *shower (with a shower)*
a *and, but*
nada *it is necessary*
atreemanteeravat' *to repair*
on *it/he*
nee rabotaeet *does not work*
na desyatam itazhe *on the tenth floor*
skol'ka *how much/how many*
tol'ka *only*
peetsot *500*
rooblee, rooblyeiy *rouble(s)*
na cheelavyeka *for a person (per person)*
kreedeetniee kartachkee *credit cards*
preeneemaeem *we accept*
zaftrak *breakfast*
s vas'mee cheesof *from eight hours (from eight o'clock)*
do, da *until*

dyeveet'/deeveetee *nine*
noo... *well...*
mi khateem *we want*
mozhna *it is possible*
zaftrakat' *to have breakfast*
syem' sorak pyat' *7.45*
ikskoorseeya *excursion*
zaftra *tomorrow*
voseem' peetnatsat *8.15*
vapros *question*
kofee *coffee*
eelee *or*
chyaiy *tea*
peet'/ya p'yu *to drink/I drink*
z'dyes' *here*
kafe *café*
atsyuda *from here*
bleeska *close, near*
nalyeva *to the left, on the left*
naprava *to the right, on the right*
treetsat myetraf *30 metres*
patom *then, next*
pryama *straight on*
slooshayu *I listen*
vi/vas *you*
nam *for us*
sakhar/sakhara *sugar*
malako/malakom *milk*
fsyo *all, everything*
bootirbrot/ bootirbrodi *sandwich/sandwiches*
sir/siram *cheese*

veetcheena/veetcheenoiy *ham*
oozhasniiy *terrible*
stol *table*
maleen'keeiy/maleen'kaya *small*

tooalyeti *toilets*
cheestiee *clean*
khalodniy *cold*
afeetsiant *waiter*
shshyot *bill*
peedeesyat *50*

TOTAL NEW WORDS: 67
…only 239 words to go!

SOME USEFUL EXTRAS

TSIFRI *(NUMERALS)*

adeenatsat' *11*	dveenatsat' *12*	treenatsat' *13*
cheetirnatsat' *14*	peetnatsat' *15*	shisnatsat' *16*
seemnatsat' *17*	vaseemnatsat *18*	deeveetnatsat' *19*
dvatsat' *20*	treetsat' *30*	sorak *40*
peedeesyat *50*	shiz'deesyat *60*	syemdeesyat *70*
voseemdeesyat *80*	deeveenosta *90*	sto *100*
dvyes'tee *200*	treesta *300*	cheetireesta *400*
peetsot *500*	shisot *600*	tiseechya *1000*

You join numbers just like in English: *23* = dvatsat' tree;
35 = treetsat pyat'.

VRYEMYA *(TELLING THE TIME)*

cheesi *clock*
f katoram cheesoo? *at what time?*
f tree cheesa *at three o'clock*
(f) syem' treetsat' (*at*) 7.30
chyas *hour*
needyelya *week*
got *year*

tree cheesa *it is three o'clock*
v dva cheesa *at two o'clock*
f pyat cheesof *at five o'clock*
meenoota *minute*
dyen' *day*
myeseets *month*

GOOD NEWS GRAMMAR

🔊 CD1, TR 12

1 DOING THINGS

In Week 1 you learned how to *say I, you, we... work* or *travel*.

Now let's complete the list with *he, she, it* and *they... work* or *are working*.

Bar**ee**s rab**o**taeet. On rab**o**taeet.	*Boris works. He is working.*
Ol'ga rab**o**taeet. An**a** rab**o**taeet.	*Olga works. She is working.*
Teelee**fo**n rab**o**taeet. On rab**o**taeet.	*The telephone works. It is working.*
Bar**ee**s ee **O**l'ga rab**o**tayut. An**ee** rab**o**tayut.	*Boris and Olga work. They are working.*

So it's -eet for one person and -yut for more than one. And if you want to use the basic form, i.e. *to work*, it's rab**o**tat' (with an apostrophe at the end).

2 TO WANT AND TO BE ABLE TO/CAN

Here are two important verbs which you'll use all the time. Unfortunately, they don't behave as well as rab**o**tat'. I have put them into gift boxes for you so you won't forget. Spend five minutes on each. Use *want* instead of *would like*. It does not sound at all rude in Russian.

khatyet' *want*	
ya khach**u**	*I want*
vi khat**ee**tee	*you want*
mi khat**ee**m	*we want*
on, an**a**, an**o** kh**o**cheet	*he, she, it wants*
an**ee** khat**ya**t	*they want*

moch' *can*	
ya mag**oo**	*I can*
vi m**o**zhite	*you can*
mi m**o**zhim	*we can*
on, an**a**, an**o** m**o**zhit	*he, she, it can*
an**ee** m**o**goot	*they can*

3 NADA: *THE 'NECESSARY' AND* MOZHNA: *THE 'POSSIBLE'*

These are two very useful words. Remember when Olga said that
the shower needed repairing:

Nada atreeman**tee**ravat'... *It is necessary to repair...*

And then Tom wondered if they could have breakfast:

Mozhna zaftrakat'? *Is it possible to have breakfast?*

When you use **nada** and **mozhna** you'll carry on with the basic
verb – just like in English. *It is necessary/possible to work/drink*:
nada/mozhna rabotat'/peet', etc.

4 WORD ORDER: VERY RELAXED!

We don't accept credit cards could be either: kreed**ee**tniee
kartachkee mi nee preeneem**a**eem or mi nee preeneem**a**eem
kreed**ee**tniye **ka**rtachkee. Take your pick!

5 NYET *AND* NYE

Everyone knows **nyet** means *no*! Its 'brother' **nye** (*not*) is used when
you are not doing something.

I don't work.	**Ya nye rab**otayu.
He's not working.	**On nye rab**otaeet.

6 ...AND NOW FOR THE BAD NEWS: ENDINGS

There are three types of nouns in Russian: masculine, feminine and
neuter. You can often identify which is which by the ending –
usually a *consonant* (masculine), an **a** (feminine) or an **o** (neuter).
The trouble starts when you use a noun in a sentence. Take **sir**:
cheese. Take *bread with cheese*: bootirbrot s siram. **Sir** changes to
siram. Adjectives and numbers behave equally badly: *new* could
be: noviy, novim, novaya and more! But don't despair. You'll pick
them up as you go along.

LET'S SPEAK RUSSIAN

Now let's practise what you have learned. I'll give you ten English sentences and you say them in Russian – out loud! If you have the recording, listen to check the answers. Tick each sentence if you got it right. Unless you got all ten correct, do the exercise again.

1 We would like a double room.
2 Unfortunately, it is too expensive.
3 Breakfast is at what time?
4 The telephone does not work.
5 We want sandwiches.
6 Do you also have tea?
7 Where is the café, left or right?
8 The toilets are not clean.
9 Can I please have the bill?
10 Tomorrow I go to London at nine o'clock.

Now answer in Russian. Use da and mi for the ones on the left and nyet and ya for the ones on the right.

11 Vi khateetee yekhat' v Maskvoo?
12 Oo vas z'dyes' teeleefon?
13 Vi khateetee yes't' (*to eat*) v voseem cheesof?
14 Vi mozhitee rabotat' zaftra?
15 Vi khateetee nomeer?

Now answer the last two using the words in brackets.

16 Gdye z'dyes' kafe? (bleeska, atsyuda)
17 F katoram cheesoo vi khateetee yes't'? (v shes't' sorak pyat)

Answers

1 *Mi khateem nomeer na dvaeekh.*

2 *K sazhilyeneeyu eta stoeet sleeshkam doraga.*

3 *Zaftrak v katoram cheesoo?*

4 *Teeleefon nye rabotaeet.*

5 *Mi khateem bootirbrodi.*

6 *A chyaiy oo vas yes't'?*

7 *Gdye kafe, nalyeva eelee naprava?*

8 *Tooalyeti nee cheestiee.*

9 *Shshyot, pazhaloosta.*

10 *Zaftra ya v Londanee v dyeveet cheesof.*

11 *Da, mi khateem yekhat' v Maskvoo.*

12 *Da, oo nas z'dyes' yes't' teeleefon.*

13 *Nyet, ya nee khachu yes't' v voseem cheesof.*

14 *Nyet, ya nee magoo rabotat' zaftra.*

15 *Nyet, ya nee khachu nomeer.*

16 *Kafe bleeska atsyuda.*

17 *Ya khachu yes't' f shes't' sorak pyat.*

LET'S SPEAK MORE RUSSIAN

🔊 **CD1, TR 14**

Here are the two optional exercises. Remember, they may stretch the 45 minutes a day by 15 minutes. But the extra practice will be worth it.

IN YOUR OWN WORDS

This exercise will teach you to express yourself freely. Use only the words you have learned so far.

Tell me in your own words that…

1 you want to know if an en suite double room is available
2 you want to know the price of the room for one night
3 you would like breakfast at 7.30
4 you would like to know where you can have a tea or a coffee
5 you have an excursion to Novgorod at 8.45
6 you want to know if the café is close by. Is it to the left and then straight ahead, 100 metres?
7 you want tea without sugar, a sandwich with cheese and a sandwich with ham

Tell me…

8 what you don't like about the café (awful tea, small table, dirty toilets)
9 that Kate says the waiter is good looking (Kate gavareet, shto… *Kate says that…*)
10 that the bill is 80 roubles

....

Answers

1 *Oo vas yes't' nomeer na dvaeekh s vanaiy ee z dooshim?*
2 *Skol'ka stoeet nomeer na adnoo noch?*
3 *Mozhna zafrakat' v syem' treetsat'?*
4 *Gdye mozhna peet' chyaiy eelee kofee?*
5 *Oo nas ikskoorseeya v Novgarat v voseem' sorak pyat.*
6 *Kafe atsyuda bleeska? Kafe nalyeva, patom naprava ee pryama sto myetraf?*
7 *Nam chyaiy bees sakhara, bootirbrot s siram ee bootirbrot s veecheenoiy, pazhaloosta.*
8 *Chyaiy oozhasniiy, stol sleeshkam maleen'keeiy ee tooalyeti nye ocheen' cheestiee.*
9 *Kate gavareet, shto afeetsiant kraseeviiy.*
10 *Shshyot – voseem'deesyat rooblyeiy.*

LET'S SPEAK RUSSIAN – FAST AND FLUENTLY

🔊 **CD1, TR 15**

Translate each section and check if it is correct. Then cover up the answers and say the three or four sentences as quickly as you can.

Try to say each group of sentences in less than 30 seconds.

Some of the English is in Russian-speak to help you.

Good evening. Do you have a room with bath?
700 roubles per person – too expensive.
I want room with shower.
How much costs breakfast?

Dobriiy vyecheer. Oo vas yes't' nomeer s vanaiy?
Seemsot rooblyeiy na cheelavyeka – sleeshkam doraga.
Ya khachu nomeer z dooshim.
Skol'ka stoeet zaftrak?

Bank from here very near, straight ahead, then right 20 metres.
Tomorrow at five o'clock we are going to Yalta. Do you also want to go to Yalta?
Is it possible to have breakfast at ten o'clock?

Bank atsyuda ocheen' bleeska, pryama, patom naprava dvatsat myetraf.
Zaftra f pyat cheesof mi yedeem v Yaltoo. Vi tozhe khateetee yekhat' v Yaltoo?
Mozhna zaftrakat v dyeseet' cheesof?

The room costs very expensive. Do you have a credit card?
My breakfast – cold and coffee – awful.
The bill, please. One hundred and five roubles.

Nomeer stoeet ocheen' doraga. Oo vas yes't' kreedeetnaya kartachka?
Moiy zaftrak khalodniy ee kofee oozhasniiy.
Shshyot, pazhaloosta. Sto pyat rooblyeiy.

Now say all the sentences in Russian without stopping and starting. If you can do it in under 90 seconds you are a fast and fluent winner!

But if you are not happy with your result – just try once more.

LEARN BY HEART

Choose one of these to fill in the gaps: **maeem moozhim** *husband*, **mayeiy zhinoiy** *wife*, **maeem droogam** *friend*, **mayeiy padroogaiy** *girlfriend*. Try to say it in under one minute.

CD1, TR 16

> **Oo meenya mala dyeneek, no...**
>
> Oo meenya mala* dyeneek, no ya khachu otpoosk v maee.
> Ya khachu yekhat' f Sankt-Peeteerboork s...
> Ya khachu f Sankt-Peeteerboorgee peet' mnoga** shampanskava ee yes't' bootirbrodi. Eta vazmozhna***? Da, eta needoraga stoeet. Tol'ka dyeseet' tiseech rooblyeiy na cheelavyeka, ee oo meenya yes't' kreedeetnaya kartachka...

*mala: *a little* **mnoga: *a lot, many* ***vazmozhna: *it is possible*

TEST YOUR PROGRESS

Translate these sentences into Russian and write them out. See what you can remember without looking at the previous pages. (Remember. Don't highlight the part of the word which is stressed.)

1 I drink a lot of champagne.
2 How much is (costs) breakfast, please?
3 Is there a travel agency here?
4 Do you have a table? At 7.15?
5 I would like to drink (some) coffee.
6 My holiday in Florida was better.
7 Where is there a good hotel?
8 Can I have the telephone bill, please?
9 We were in Saint Petersburg in May.
10 My house is too big.
11 At what time are you in Moscow tomorrow?
12 I am there from eight until five.
13 Excuse me, please. Where are the toilets, straight ahead?
14 We want to travel to Oslo in January, but it is too cold.
15 Does that cost more money?
16 Tomorrow where are you at 10.30?
17 It's terrible. The (hotel) room is very expensive.
18 Is it possible to drink coffee here now? Do you have seats?
19 We have a small house in America, but it is very expensive.
20 Goodbye, we are going to Yalta.

Check your answers and work out your score. Now enter your result on the **Progress chart** in the front of the book. If it is above 70% you have done very well.

3

Week three

DAY-BY-DAY GUIDE

Study for 45 minutes a day – but there are no penalties for doing more!

DAY ONE

▶ Read **Let's go shopping**.
▶ Listen to/Read **Mi dyelaeem pakoopkee**.
▶ Listen to/Read the **New words**, then learn some of them.

DAY TWO

▶ Repeat **Mi dyelaeem pakoopkee** and the **New words**.
▶ Learn all the **New words**. Use the **Flash cards**.

DAY THREE

▶ Test yourself on all the **New words** – boring perhaps, but you are over halfway already.
▶ Read and learn the **Good news grammar**.
▶ Go over the **Good news grammar**.

DAY FOUR

▶ Listen to/Read **Learn by heart**.
▶ Cut out and learn the ten **Flash sentences**.

DAY FIVE

▶ Listen to/Read **Spot the keys**.
▶ Listen to/Read **Let's speak Russian**.

DAY SIX

▶ Go over **Learn by heart**.
▶ Have a quick look at **New words**, Weeks 1–3. You now know over 200 words! Well, more or less.
▶ Listen to/Read **Let's speak more Russian** (optional).
▶ Listen to/Read **Let's speak Russian – fast and fluently** (optional).
▶ Translate **Test your progress**.

DAY SEVEN

Enjoy your day off!

LET'S GO SHOPPING

Tom and Kate are staying in Moscow. Kate is planning some shopping. Don't forget that the English is in 'Russian-speak' to help you get used to the way the language works.

Kate Well, today for us it is necessary to do shopping. First we go to centre of town on bus.

Tom But weather bad. (It is) Cold. And on television much sport. At 12.30 goes (is on) golf…

Kate Sorry, but for us it is necessary (to go) to bank, to post office for stamps, to chemist's, to dry cleaner's and to supermarket.

Tom Well, golf not possible to watch… perhaps football at three o'clock. Is that all?

Kate No, for us it is necessary also (to go) to department store for new suitcase and to hairdresser's. And I want also (to go) to jewellery shop and to shop of souvenirs.

Tom Good grief! Shops open until what time?

Kate Until six or until eight, it seems.

Tom Ah, football also not possible to watch… perhaps tennis at 8.30…

(Later…)

Kate It seems, I too many presents bought. Bottle of champagne, tin of caviar, Russian dolls, chocolate.

Tom No problem! For us it is necessary to buy many presents. But what there, in big bag? Is it for me?

Kate And yes and no. I was in jewellery shop, then in department store. In jewellery shop I saw brooch. It is amber brooch. Splendid, isn't it true? Shop assistant was very pleasant and so handsome as Tom Cruise.

Tom Who such (who is) Tom Cruise? And how much costs brooch?

Kate A little expensive… 600 roubles.

Tom What?… Crazy!

Kate But here is T-shirt. It costs not very expensive. And here's English newspaper… and on television now is going (is on) tennis, isn't it true?

MI DYELAEEM PAKOOPKEE

Tom and Kate are staying in Moscow. Kate is planning some shopping.

Kate   Noo, seevodnya nam nada dyelat' pakoopkee. Snachyala mi **ye**deem f tsentr gorada na avtoboosee.

Tom   No pagoda plakhaya. Kholadna. Ee po teeleeveezaroo mnoga sporta. V dveenatsat treetsat eedyot gol'f...

Kate   Ezveenee, no nam nada v bank, na pochtoo za markamee, v aptyekoo, f kheemcheestkoo ee f soopeermarkeet.

Tom   Noo, gol'f neel'zya smatryet'... mozhit bit' footbol f tree cheesa. Eta fsyo?

Kate   Nyet, nam nada tozhe v ooneeveermak za novim cheemadanam ee f pareekmakheerskooyu. Ee ya khachu v yuveeleerniy magazeen ee v magazeen sooveeneeraf.

Tom   Bozhe moiy! Magazeeni atkriti da kakova chyasa?

Kate   Da shes't'ee eelee da vas'mee, kazhitsa.

Tom   Akh, foodbol tozhe neel'zya smatryet'... mozhit bit' tenees v voseem' treetsat'...

(Later...)

Kate   Kazhetsa, ya sleeshkam mnoga padarkaf koopeela. Bootilkoo shampanskava, bankoo eekri, matryoshkee, shikalat.

Tom   Nyet prablyem! Nam nada koopeet' mnoga padarkaf. A shto tam v balshoiy soomkee? Eta dlya meenya?

Kate   Ee da ee nyet. Ya bila v yuveeleernam magazeenee, patom v ooneeveermagee. V yuveeleernam magazeenee ya ooveedeela broshkoo. Eta yantarnaya broshka. Preekrasnaya, nye pravda lee? Pradavyets bil ocheen' preeyatniiy ee takoiy zhe krasaveets, kak Tom Cruise.

Tom   Kto takoiy Tom Cruise? Ee skol'ka stoeet broshka?

Kate   Neemnoshka doraga. Shisot (600) rooblyeiy.

Tom   Shto? S ooma sashla!

Kate   No vot foodbolka. Stoeet nye ocheen' doraga. A vot angleeskaya gazyeta... a po teeleeveezaroo seechyas eedyot tenees, nye pravda lee?

NEW WORDS

◀) CD1, TR 18

Learn the **New words** in half the time using the **Flash cards** at the back of the book. There are 22 to start you off.

seevodnya *today*
dyelat' *to do*
pakoopkee *the shopping*
snachyala *first*
tsentr *centre*
aftoboos/aftoboosee *bus*
pagoda *weather*
plakhaya *bad*
kholadna *cold*
po, pa *on, along, according to*
teeleeveezar/teeleeveezaroo *television*
sport/sporta/sportoo *sport*
eedyot *(he, she) it goes, is going*
eezveenee *I am sorry (informal)*
pochta/pochtoo *post office*
za *for, behind, beyond*
markee/markamee *stamps*
aptyeka/aptyekoo *chemist's*
kheemcheestka/kheemcheestkoo *dry cleaner's*
soopeermarkeet *supermarket*
neel'zya *it is not possible, one may not*
smatryet' *to watch*
mozhit bit' *perhaps*
f tree cheesa *at three o'clock*
ooneeveermag/ooneeveermagee *department store*
noviy/novim *new*

cheemadan/cheemadanam *suitcase*
pareekmakheerskaya/pareekmakheerskooyu *hairdresser's*
yuveleerniy *jewellery*
magazeen/magazeenee *shop/shops*
sooveeneeri/sooveeneeraf *souvenirs*
Bozhe moiy! *Good grief! (lit: God my!)*
atkriti *open (plural form)*
da kakova chyasa? *until when?*
kazhitsa *it seems, I think/believe*
tenees *tennis*
mnoga *many*
koopeela (I) *bought*
bootilkoo shampanskava *bottle (of) champagne*
shampanskaye *champagne*
padarkee/padarkaf *presents*
banka/bankoo *tin, jar*
eekra/eekri *caviar*
matryoshka/matryoshkee *Russian doll/dolls*
shikalat *chocolate*
nyet prablyem! *no problem!*
koopeet'/koopeela *to buy/she bought*
shto *what, that*

soomka, soomkee/pakyeteek
  bag
dlya meenya for me
ooveedeet'/ooveedeela to see/
  she saw
broshka/broshkoo brooch
yantarnaya amber
preekrasnaya splendid
nye pravda lee isn't it?
pradavyets shop assistant
preeyatniiy pleasant

takoiy zhe … kak just as … as
krasaveets handsome fellow
kto takoiy… ? Who is… ?
neemnoshka a little
s ooma sashla crazy! (to a man
  one would say: s ooma sashol)
vot here (there) is/are
foodbolka T-shirt
angleeskaya/Angleeya,
  Anglee-ee English/England
gazyeta newspaper

TOTAL NEW WORDS: 67
…only 172 words to go!

MORE EXTRAS

TSVEETA (COLOURS)

byeliiy	white	zeelyoniiy	green
chyorniiy	black	aranzhiviiy	orange
krasniiy	red	rozaviiy	pink
seeneey	blue	syeriiy	grey
zholtiiy	yellow	kareechneeviiy	brown

SPOT THE KEYS

◀ CD1, TR 19

By now you can say many things in Russian. But what happens if you ask a question and don't understand the answer – hitting you at the speed of a machine gun? The smart way is not to panic, but to listen out for the words you know. Any familiar words which you pick up will provide you with key words – clues to what the other person is saying.

If you have the recording listen to the dialogue. If you don't – read on. You are trying to ask the way to the post office…

You	Eezveeneetee, pazh**a**loosta, gdye p**o**chta?
Answer	*Noo, eta nye tak prosta. Snachyala eedeetee* pry**a**ma da *slyedooshcheevapeereekryostka, tamgdyenakhodeetsa* balsh**o**iy kr**a**sniiy dom. Pat**o**m nal**ye**va, *vi ooveedeetee tam eeshshyo* magaz**ee**ni. *Eeshshyopadalshye eedeetye naprava. Vi ooveedeetee* apt**ye**koo *naproteef pochti*.

Did you hear the key words? **pryama da – balshoiy krasniiy dom – patom – nalyeva – magazeeni – aptyekoo – pochti.**

GOOD NEWS GRAMMAR

◀) CD1, TR 20

1 *THE PAST*

This is easier than in French! Here's a very basic 'recipe:

▶ Take the basic form of the verb, say, **rabotat**.
▶ Take off the **t** and add an **l** if you are talking about
  one male person (it could be Boris or yourself): **Barees rabotal**.
▶ Add **la** for one female person (it could be Tanya or you):
  Tanya rabotala.
▶ Add **lo** for neuter nouns: **radeea ne rabotalo** (pronounced
  rabotala).
▶ Add **lee** for *you* (**vi**) and everything that's more than one: *Boris
  and Tanya, we, they...* **rabotalee**.

Most important: learn all the sample phrases which are in the past.

2 NADA, MOZHNA *AND* NEEL'ZYA

Remember **nada** and **mozhna** from Week 2? *It is necessary. It is
possible.* Here's another one: **neel'zya**: *it's forbidden,* so *it's not possible.*

These three are very useful when you want to say *can, can't* or *must,*
because that's really what they express: *I can... for me it's possible.
I can't... for me it's not possible. I must... for me it's necessary.*

So all you need to do now is to add: *for me, for you, for us,* etc.
Here's the full list using **nada** and *must buy* as an example:

mnye **nada** koop**ee**t'	*for me it is necessary... I must buy*
vam **nada** koop**ee**t'	*for you it is necessary... you must buy*
nam **nada** koop**ee**t'	*for us it is necessary... we must buy*
yem**oo**/yeiy **nada** koop**ee**t'	*for him/her it is necessary... he/she must buy*
eem **nada** koop**ee**t'	*for them it is necessary... they must buy.*

So now you can mix and match. Mnye m**o**zhna koop**ee**t: *I can buy.*
Nam neel'z**ya** rabotat: *We can't work.*

3 *'TO GO'*: EETEE' *'ON FOOT'* AND YEKHAT' *'BY TRANSPORT'*

We've put these two useful verbs in a box to help you
remember them.

eet**ee**'			**ye**khat'	
ya eed**oo**	*I go*		ya **ye**doo	
vi eed**yo**tee	*you go*		vi **ye**deetee	
on, an**a** eed**yo**t	*he, she goes*		on, an**a** **ye**deet	
mi eed**yom**	*we go*		mi **ye**deem	
an**ee** eed**oo**t	*they go*		an**ee** **ye**doot	

LEARN BY HEART

Say these seven lines in under 50 seconds. The more expression you
use the easier it will be to remember all the useful bits.

> Seev**o**dnya nam n**a**da d**ye**lat' pak**oo**pkee – nyet prabl**ye**m!
> No atk**oo**da* **ye**deet aft**o**boos v magaz**ee**ni?
> Akh, b**o**zhe moiy! K**a**zhitsa, oo meen**ya** mala d**ye**neek.
> Mi koop**ee**lee mn**o**ga pad**a**rkaf: matr**yo**shkee, br**o**shkoo ee b**a**nkoo eekri.
> **E**ta bila d**o**roga: shessot roobl**yeiy**, no pradav**ye**ts bil **o**cheen' pree**ya**tniy.

*atk**oo**da: *from where*

LET'S SPEAK RUSSIAN

◀) CD2, TR 2

Over to you. If you have the recording, listen to check your answers. Always answer out loud. Start with a ten-point warm-up. Say in Russian:

1 Now I am going to (the) post office.
2 Until what time (are the) shops open?
3 I am sorry, but that is too expensive.
4 From where bus goes to centre?
5 We bought souvenirs in Novgorod.
6 Can one buy caviar in the supermarket?
7 Shopping without money? No, but I have (a) credit card.
8 I everything bought in the department store.
9 We must watch the weather on television.
10 Good grief! The television doesn't work!

Answer the following using the words in brackets.

11 Oo vas yes't' seenee-ee foodbolkee? (da, oo nas)
12 Vi koopeelee markee f soopeermarkeetee? (da, mi)
13 Vi rabotalee v bankee? (nyet, mi)
14 Vam nada eetee v dyeveet cheesof? (nyet, nam)
15 Oo vas mnoga dyeneek? (nyet, oo nas, mala)
16 Shto vi koopeelee? Shikalat eelee shampanskaye? (shikalat)
17 Kto smatryel foodbol po teeleeveezaroo? (ya)
18 Da kakova chyasa magazeenee atkriti? (vas'mee cheesof)

Answers

1 *Seechyas ya eedoo na pochtoo.*

2 *Magazeeni atkriti da kakova chyasa?*

3 *Ezveeneetee no eta sleeshkam doraga.*

4 *Atkooda aftoboos yedeet f tsentr?*

5 *Mi koopeelee sooveeneeri v Novgaradee.*

6 *Mozhna koopeet' eekroo f soopeermarkeetee?*

7 *Dyelat' pakoopkee bees dyeneek? Nyet, no oo meenya yes't' kreedeetnaya kartachka.*

8 *Ya fsyo koopeela f ooneeveermagee.*

9 *Nam nada smatryet' pagodoo po teeleeveezaroo.*

10 *Bozhe moiy! Teeleeveezar nee rabotaeet!*

11 *Da, oo nas yes't' seenee-ee foodbolkee.*

12 *Da, mi koopeelee markee f soopeermarkeetee.*

13 *Nyet, mi nee rabotalee v bankee.*

14 *Nyet, nam nee nada eetee f dyeveet cheesof.*

15 *Nyet, oo nas mala dyeneek.*

16 *Mi koopeelee (ya koopeel/ya koopeela) shikalat.*

17 *Ya smatryel/ya smatryela foodbol po teeleeveezaroo.*

18 *Da vas'mee (cheesof).*

LET'S SPEAK MORE RUSSIAN

◄» CD2, TR 3

Here are the two optional exercises. Remember, they may stretch the 45 minutes a day by 15 minutes. But the extra practice will be worth it.

IN YOUR OWN WORDS

This exercise will teach you to express yourself freely. Use only the words you have learned so far.

Tell me in your own words that...

1 today you must go shopping
2 first you are going to the centre of town by bus
3 unfortunately you have little money, but you do have a credit card
4 you have to go to the supermarket to buy a bottle of champagne
5 then you have to go to the department store to buy Russian dolls
6 you bought caviar, coffee and chocolate in the supermarket
7 it was very expensive; it seems now you have little money
8 you watched the weather on television
9 the sandwiches cost 15 roubles; that was not expensive
10 you have bought too many presents

....

Answers

1 *Seevodnya mnye nada dyelat' pakoopkee.*

2 *Snachyala ya yedoo f tsentr gorada na aftoboosee.*

3 *K sazhilyeneeu oo meenya mala dyeneek, no oo meenya kreedeetnaya kartachka.*

4 *Mnye nada v soopeermarkeet koopeet' bootilkoo shampanskava.*

5 *Patom mnye nada v ooneeveermak koopeet' matryoshkee.*

6 *Ya koopeel/koopeela eekroo, kofee ee shikalat f soopeermarkeetee.*

7 *Eta bila ocheen' doraga. Kazhitsa, seechyas oo meenya mala dyeneek.*

8 *Ya smatryel/smatryela pagodoo po teeleeveezaroo.*

9 *Bootirbrodi stoeelee peetnatsat rooblyeiy. Eta bila nyedoraga.*

10 *Ya sleeshkam mnoga podarkaf koopeel/koopeela.*

LET'S SPEAK RUSSIAN – FAST AND FLUENTLY

◄) CD2, TR 4

Translate each section and check if it is correct. Then cover up the answers and say the three or four sentences as quickly as you can. Some of the English is in 'Russian-speak' to help you. Try to say each section in less than 30 seconds.

Good grief! Is that an English newspaper?
Do you want to watch football or tennis?
Did you watch the sport on the television?

Bozhe moiy! **E**ta angl**ee**skaya gaz**ye**ta?
Vi khat**ee**tee smatr**yet**' foodb**o**l **ee**lee t**e**nees?
Vi smatr**ye**li sport po teel**ee**v**ee**zaroo?

From where bus goes to university?
Excuse me, are you going to the pharmacy?
Where can I buy stamps?
We must buy souvenirs in department store.

Atk**oo**da aft**o**boos eed**yo**t v oon**ee**v**ee**rseet**ye**t?
Eezveen**ee**tee, vi eed**yo**tee v apt**ye**koo?
Gdye m**o**zhna koop**ee**t' m**a**rkee?
Nam n**a**da koop**it**' soov**ee**n**ee**ri v oon**ee**v**ee**rm**a**gee.

Today the weather is good.
I don't need to go at six o'clock.
Today you mustn't work. You must go shopping.

Seev**o**dnya pag**o**da khar**o**shaya.
Mnye nee n**a**da eet**ee** f shes't' chees**o**f.
Seev**o**dnya vam neel'**zya** rab**o**tat'. Vam n**a**da d**ye**lat' pak**oo**pkee.

Now say all the sentences in Russian without stopping and starting. If you can do it all in under 90 seconds you are a fast and fluent winner. But if you are not happy with your result – just try once more.

TEST YOUR PROGRESS

Translate the following sentences into Russian and write them down. Then check your answers and be amazed.

1 Where is (the) sales assistant?
2 Where is it possible to buy sandwiches?
3 When must you (go) to England today? At seven o'clock?
4 We saw that yesterday on television.
5 Now (the) shops (are) open, it seems.
6 Here there is (a) department store or supermarket?
7 Excuse me, are you also going to the post office?
8 Where did you buy (the) English newspaper?
9 Do you want coffee or tea?
10 The weather is bad today. It is not possible to go to Novgorod.
11 That is all? That was not expensive.
12 The stamps cost 15 roubles.
13 We accept credit cards.
14 Is 300 grams (of) cheese too much? No, no problem.
15 There is (a) new dry cleaner's near here.
16 Do you have (a) bag for my T-shirt, please?
17 I saw here (a) chemist's, it seems.
18 Good grief! (The) bus has broken down (isn't working) and (the) Mercedes also has broken down (isn't working)!
19 Did you see (the) T-shirt? Where did you buy it?
20 Five hundred roubles, but I have only dollars.

Remember to fill in the **Progress chart**. You are now halfway home!

4

Week four

DAY-BY-DAY GUIDE

Study for 45 minutes a day but if you are keen try 50... 55...!

DAY ONE

- ▶ Read **We are going to the restaurant.**
- ▶ Listen to/Read **Mi eedyom v reestaran.**
- ▶ Read the **New words**. Learn the easy ones.

DAY TWO

- ▶ Repeat the dialogue. Learn the harder **New words**.
- ▶ Cut out the **Flash words** to help you.

DAY THREE

- ▶ Learn all the **New words** until you know them well.
- ▶ Read and learn the **Good news grammar**.

DAY FOUR

- ▶ Listen to/Read **Learn by heart**.
- ▶ Cut out and learn the ten **Flash sentences**.

DAY FIVE

▶ Listen to/Read **Spot the keys**.
▶ Read **Say it simply**.

DAY SIX

▶ Listen to/Read **Let's speak Russian**.
▶ Listen to/Read **Let's speak more Russian** (optional).
▶ Listen to/Read **Let's speak Russian – fast and fluently** (optional).
▶ Translate **Test your progress**.

DAY SEVEN

Are you keeping your scores above 60%? In that case... have a good day off!

WE ARE GOING TO (THE) RESTAURANT

Tom and Kate are still in Moscow. Boris Vadimovich invites them to dinner.

Don't forget that the English is in 'Russian-speak' to help you get used to the way the language works.

Kate	Tom, someone rang. He did not say why. Number is on paper, by telephone. Some Boris…
Tom	Oh, yes, Boris Vadimovich, good customer of our firm. I him well know. Very pleasant person. By me meeting with him on Thursday. Very important matter.
Tom	*(On the phone...)* Hello, good morning, Boris Vadimovich… Speaks Tom Walker… Yes, thank you… yes, of course, it is possible… next week… of course… yes… very interesting… no, by us time there is… splendid… no, only for a few days… I understand… when?… at 8 o'clock… upstairs by exit, by door. Well, until Tuesday, thank you very much, goodbye.
Kate	What are we doing on Tuesday?
Tom	We are going to restaurant with Boris Vadimovich. Restaurant in centre behind church. He says, that restaurant new. Boris Vadimovich in Moscow for two days, with Edith and Peter Palmer from our firm.
Kate	I know Edith Palmer. She is boring and knows everything. She has a terrible dog. I think, that on Tuesday I will be ill. Heavy cold and everything hurts. The doctor necessary it will be to call…
Tom	Please, (one can't do that) thus it is not possible; it's not on. Boris Vadimovich is very important client.

MI EEDYOM V REESTARAN

Tom and Kate are still in Moscow. Boris Vadimovich invites them to dinner.

Kate	Tom, kto-ta pazvaneel. On nee skazal, pacheemoo. Nomeer na boomagee, okala teeleefona. Kakoiy-ta Barees.
Tom	Akh, da, Barees Vadeemaveech, kharoshiiy kleeyent nashiiy feermi. Ya yeevo kharasho znayu. Ocheen' preeyatniy cheelavyek. Oo meenya fstryechya s neem f cheetvyerk. Ocheen' vazhniee deela.
Tom	*(On the phone...)* Alo, dobraye ootra, Barees Vadeemaveech. Gavareet Tom Walker... Da, spaseeba... da, kanyeshna vazmozhna... na slyedooshshyeeiy needyele... kanyeshna... da... ocheen' eenteeryesna... nyet, oo nas vryemya yes't'... preekrasna... nyet, tol'ka na nyeskal'ka dnyeiy... Ya paneemayu... kagda?... v voseem' cheesof... naveerkhoo, okala vikhada, okala dveeree. Noo, do ftorneeka, spaseeba balshoye, da sveedaneeya.
Kate	Shto mi dyelaeem va ftorneek?
Tom	Mi eedyom v reestaran s Bareesam Vadeemaveecheem. Reestaran f tsentree, za tserkav'yu. On gavareet, shto reestaran noviy. Barees Vadeemaveech v Maskvye na dva dnya, s Edith i Peeterom Palmer eez nashiiy feermi.
Kate	Ya znayu Edith Palmer. Ana skoochnaya ee fsyo znayet loochshye vsyekh. Oo neeyo oozhasnaya sabaka. Ya doomayu, shto va ftorneek ya boodoo bal'na. Prastooda ee fsyo baleet. Vrachya nada boodeet vizvat'...
Tom	Pazhalusta, tak neel'zya, tak nye gadeetsa. Barees Vadeemaveech ocheen' vazhniiy kleeyent.

(In the restaurant...)

Waiter Here's the menu. Today by us also firm's dishes
(specials) – fish, and for sweet course – walnut cake.

Boris What for you, Mrs Walker? Soup you want?
Meat or fish?

Kate For me steak with salad, please.

Edith To eat much red meat is harmful, Kate.

Boris Mr Walker, what for you? And what you want to drink?
Wine?

Tom Beer, then sausage with fried potato, please.

Edith But Tom, that's very greasy! I would not want to eat such
dishes.

Boris And you, Mrs Palmer?

Edith Small piece of chicken from grill, fruit and glass of
water.

(Later...)

Boris Everyone ready? It is already late. Who wants coffee?
No one? Good, bill, please.

Edith Oh, Boris Vadimovich, you can me help, please?
How in Russian 'doggy bag'? I want bag for
my dog.

Kate But Edith, your dog in England!

(In the restaurant...)

Waiter   Vot meen**yu**. Seev**o**dnya oo nas t**o**zhe f**ee**rmeeniee bl**yu**da – r**i**ba, ee na sl**a**tkaye – ar**ye**khaviy tort.

Boris   Shto vam, gaspazh**a** Walker? Soop khat**ee**tee? M**ya**sa **ee**lee rib**oo**?

Kate   Mnye beefsht**e**ks s sal**a**tam, pazh**a**loosta.

Edith   Yes't' mn**o**ga t**yo**mnava m**ya**sa vr**ye**dna, Kate.

Boris   Gaspad**ee**n Walker, shto vam? Ee shto vi khat**ee**tye peet'? Veen**o**?

Tom   P**ee**va, pat**o**m kalbas**oo** z zh**a**reenaiy kart**o**shkaiy, pazh**a**loosta.

Edith   No Tom, **e**ta **o**cheen' zh**i**rna! Ya nye khat**ye**la bi yes't' tak**o**ye bl**yu**da.

Boris   A vi, gaspazh**a** Palmer?

Edith   M**a**leenkiy koos**o**chyek k**oo**reetsi, z gr**ee**lya, fr**oo**kti ee stak**a**n vad**i**.

(Later...)

Boris   Fsye gat**o**vi? Oozh**e** p**o**zna. Kto kh**o**cheet k**o**fee? Neekt**o**? Kharash**o**, shshyot, pazh**a**loosta.

Edith   Akh, Bar**ee**s Vad**ee**maveech, vi nee m**o**zhitee mnye pam**o**ch, pazh**a**loosta? Kak pa-r**oo**skee 'doggy bag'? Ya khach**u** pak**ye**teek dlya ma**yeiy** sab**a**kee.

Kate   No Edith, v**a**sha sab**a**ka v **A**nglee-ee!

NEW WORDS

🔊 CD2, TR 6

kto-ta *someone*
pazvaneet'/pazvaneel
  to ring/he rang
on/yevo/neem *he, him*
skazat'/skazal *to say/he said*
pachemoo *why*
nomeer *number*
boomaga/boomagee *paper*
okala *near, by*
kakoiy-ta *some (sort of)*
kleeyent *customer*
kharasho *good, well*
feerma/feermi *firm*
znat'/znayu/znaeet *to know/*
  I know/he/(she) knows
cheelavyek *person*
fstryechya *meeting*
cheetvyerk *Thursday*
vazhniee *important*
dyela *matter*
gavareet'/gavareet *to speak,*
  to say/he speaks, he says
spaseeba/balshoiye
  thank you/very much
kanyeshna *of course*
vazmozhna *it is possible*
slyedooshshyeeiy *next*
eenteeryesna
  it is interesting
vryemya *time*
nyeskal'ka *a few*
dnyeiy/dnya *days*

kagda *when*
naveerkhoo *upstairs*
vikhad/vikhada *exit*
dvyer/dveeree *door*
ftorneek/ftorneeka *Tuesday*
tserkaf'/tserkav'yu *church*
oozhasnaya *terrible*
sabaka *dog*
doomat'/doomayu
  to think/I think
boodoo/boodeet
  I will be/he (she, it) will be
bal'na *ill, sick*
prastooda *a cold*
baleet *it hurts*
vrach/vrachya *doctor*
vizvat'... *to summon,*
  call, send for
tak *thus, so*
nee gadeetsa *it does not*
  fit (it's not on)
meenyu *menu*
feermeeniee blyuda
  firm's dishes (i.e. specials)
riba/riboo *fish*
slatkaye *sweet, dessert*
aryekhaviy tort *walnut cake*
gaspazha *Mrs*
soop *soup*
myasa *meat*
beefshteks *steak*
salat/salatam *salad*

62

tyomnava m**ya**sa *dark (red) meat*	k**oo**reetsa/k**oo**reetsi *chicken*
vryedna *it is harmful*	gr**ee**l'/gr**ee**lya *grill*
gaspad**ee**n *Mr*	fr**oo**kt *fruit*
v**ee**no *wine*	st**a**kan *glass*
p**ee**va *beer*	vad**a**/v**a**di *water*
kalb**a**sa/kalbas**oo** *sausage*	g**a**tovi *ready*
zh**a**reenaiy kart**o**shkaiy *fried potato*	**oo**zhe *already*
zh**i**rna *it is greasy*	p**o**zna *it is late*
k**oo**s**o**cheek *piece*	n**ee**kto *no one*
	pam**o**ch' *to help*
	kak pa-r**oo**skee *how in Russian*

TOTAL NEW WORDS: 74
...only 98 words to go!

LAST EXTRAS

DAYS OF THE WEEK

paneed**ye**l'neek	*Monday*	p**ya**tneetsa	*Friday*
ft**o**rneek	*Tuesday*	soob**o**ta	*Saturday*
sr**ee**da	*Wednesday*	vaskreesy**e**n'ye	*Sunday*
cheetv**ye**rk	*Thursday*		

To say: *on Monday/Tuesday/Wednesday...*, etc. you add **f** (or **va** for *Tuesday*): **f** paneed**ye**l'neek, **va** ft**o**rneek, **f** sr**ye**doo, **f** cheetv**ye**rk, **f** p**ya**tneetsoo, **f** soob**o**too, **v** vaskreesy**e**n'ye. Some of the endings change... Spot the differences!

GOOD NEWS GRAMMAR

1 PRONOUNS – USEFUL!

These are worth learning because you'll need them all the time.

I = ya	*me* = mee**nya**	*to/for me* = mnye	*with me* = sa mnoiy
you = vi	*you* = vas	*to/for you* = vam	*with you* = s v**a**mee
he = on	*him* = yeev**o**	*to/for him* = yem**oo**	*with him* = s neem
she = an**a**	*her*= yee**yo**	*to/for her* = yeiy	*with her* = s nyeiy
we = mi	*us* = nas	*to/for us* = nam	*with us* = s n**a**mee
they = an**ee**	*them* = eekh	*to for them*= eem	*with them* = s n**ee**mee

Learn one row at a time – down or across. Then put each word on a flash card and invest ten minutes a day. By the end of the week you'll know the lot!

2 THE FUTURE – EASY!

If you want to talk about something that is going to happen in the future, you could get away with using the present tense.

Mi **ye**deem f tsentr.	*We are going to the centre/We'll go to the centre.*
Seevodnya ya ee**doo** f reestar**a**n.	*Today I am going (will go) to the restaurant.*

But if you want to say: *I'll*, *you'll*, or *he'll be...*, you say: **ya boo**doo, on **boo**deet, vi **boo**deetye:

Va ftorneek ya **boo**doo bal'n**a**.	*On Tuesday I will be ill.*

64

3 I WOULD – WOULD YOU?

To say *would* in Russian is fairly simple. Let's say:
I would buy…

You take the past tense of *buy*: *bought* = **koopeela** – and add the word **bi**:

Ya koop**ee**la bi…	*I would buy…*
An**a** khat**ye**la bi…	*She would like…*
Bar**ee**s skaz**a**l bi…	*Boris would say…*

4 SHORT CUT – LEAVING OUT THE VERB 'TO GO'

There's another bonus when using **nada**, **mozhna** or **neelz'ya**.

When you say that *it's necessary, possible or not possible to go somewhere* you can leave out the *go*: **Nam nada v bank**. *It's necessary for us (to go) to the bank*. Good shortcut!

5 BEING POLITE

If you ask a question and want to be polite you use the negative. So, instead of asking: *Could you help me?*, you'll say *You could not help me, (by any chance, could you)?* i.e. **Vi nee mozhitee mnye pamoch'?**

Vi nee znaeetee, gdye komnata 3?	*You don't know where room 3 is (by any chance, do you)?*

6 NA, DO, PO, S, V, ZA: *LOTS FOR THE PRICE OF A FEW!*

These little words which tell you where things are (also known as prepositions) are most generous: each one has several meanings. Take **na**. It can mean: *on, onto, to, at* and *for*. Here are some others:

do, da	*until, before, as far as*	s, z	*with, from*
po, pa	*along, on, according to*	v, f, va	*in, into, to, at*
za	*for, beyond, behind*		

Unfortunately, these prepositions do terrible things to the ending of the next word. But don't worry, you'll remember those when you learn your **Flash sentences** and **Learn by heart**.

LEARN BY HEART

This is a telephone call by a rather opinionated person... When you have learned it by heart try to act it out in less than a minute.

CD2, TR 8

> **Vi khateetee eetee sa mnoiy v reestaran?**
>
> Ya zn**a**yu ad**ee**n **o**cheen' khar**o**shiiy reestar**a**n.
>
> Tam m**o**zhna **o**cheen' vk**oo**sna* payes't' ee veen**o** preekr**a**snaye.
>
> Nyet, vi nee khat**ee**tye? Pacheem**oo** nyet? Ya **o**cheen' eenteer**ye**sniiy cheelav**ye**k!
>
> Vi meen**ya** nee zn**a**eetee?
>
> No kan**ye**shna, vi v**ee**deetee** meen**ya** po teeleev**ee**zaroo.
>
> Vi ne m**o**zhitee? Pacheem**oo** nyet?
>
> Oo vas v**a**zhnaye fstr**ye**chya?
>
> **E**ta neevazm**o**zhna!

*fk**oo**sna: *delicious* (the most commonly used word in Russian when praising food)

** v**ee**deet'/v**ee**deetee: *to see/you see*

66

SPOT THE KEYS

This time you are in a department store and ask the sales assistant if the red T-shirt you fancy is also available in a size 40 (sarakavova razmyera).

You   Eezveeneeti, pazhaloosta, oo vas yes't' eta foodbolka sarakavova razmyera?

She says **nyet**, then **meenootachkoo, pazhaloosta** and goes into the stockroom. When she comes back, this is what she says:

Answer   *Noo, oonas takikh foodbolok astayotsaocheen'mala, oo nas seeychas tol'ka zholtiee sarakavova razmyera. Noo oonasyes't'yeeshshyo krosniye foodbolkee treetsat' vas'mova razmyera. Ee stil'takoiy, shtoyabiskazala, shto treetsat' vas'moiy razmyer vam gadeetsa.*

Did you get the key words? Size 40 was only available in yellow. They have red in 38, which should fit.

SAY IT SIMPLY

When people want to speak Russian but don't dare, it's usually because they are trying to translate what they want to say from English into Russian. And when they don't know some of the words, they give up!

With **Fast-track Russian** you work around the words you don't know with the words you do know! Believe me, with some 400 words you can say anything! It may not always be very elegant, but you are communicating!

Here are two examples showing you how to say things in a simple way. Words that are not part of the **fast-track** vocabulary are in **bold**.

1 You need to **change** your **flight** from Tuesday to Friday.

Mi nye mozhim **ye**khat' va **f**torneek. Mi khat**ee**m samal**yo**t f **pya**tneetsoo.
We cannot travel on Tuesday. We want (an) aeroplane on Friday.

or

Ftorneek nam nee gad**ee**tsa. Mi khat**ee**m **ye**khat' f **pya**tneetsoo.
Tuesday does not fit (suit). We want to travel on Friday.

2 Your **watch** is **broken** and you need to have it mended before you leave.

Eezveen**ee**tee, pazhaloosta, nada atr**ee**manteeravat' cheesi, anee nee rabotayut. Z'dyes' yes't' magaz**ee**n, gdye mozhna skar**ye**ye atr**ee**manteeravat' eekh?

Excuse me please, it is necessary to repair clock not working. Here is there shop where possible in a hurry repair them?

LET'S SPEAK RUSSIAN

🔊 **CD2, TR 9**

Here are ten sentences to warm-up, and then on to greater things.

1 Who has said that?
2 I don't know why.
3 You to help? (can I help you?)
4 We have time – on Monday, I believe.
5 I want to drive to Moscow.
6 He would like to know that.
7 Work on Sunday? That's not on!
8 Do you want my number?
9 Chicken for me, please.
10 Yes, of course, I have an appointment.

Now pretend you are in Russia with friends who do not speak Russian. They will want you to ask people things in Russian, such as *Please ask him...*

11 if he knows Edith Palmer.
12 if he is going to the restaurant with us on Tuesday.
13 if she would like meat or fish and fried potato.
14 if they have an appointment today.
15 if they know where the restaurant is.

Now your friends ask you to tell people things. This time there may be words you don't know, so you have to use your **fast-track** words. They say: *Please tell her...*

16 that the soup is very delicious.
17 that unfortunately the shower is not in working order.
18 that we would like a meal with them.
19 that you are allergic to fish.
20 that Saturday will suit us.

Answers

1 *Kto skazal eta?*
2 *Ya ne znayu, pacheemoo.*
3 *Vam pamoch'?*
4 *Oo nas vryemya yes't' – f paneedyel'neek, kazhitsa.*
5 *Ya khachu yekhat' v Maskvoo.*
6 *On khatyel bi znat' eta.*
7 *Rabotat' v vaskreesyen'ye? Tak nye gadeetsa!*
8 *Vi khateetee moiy nomeer?*
9 *Mnye kooreetsoo, pazhaloosta.*
10 *Da, kanyeshna, oo meenya fstryechya.*
11 *Vi znaeetee Edith Palmer?*
12 *Vi eedyotee s namee v reestaran va ftorneek?*
13 *Vi khateetee myasa eelee riboo z zhareenaiy kartoshkaiy?*
14 *Yes't' oo vas fstryechya seevodnya.*
15 *Vi nee znaeetee, gdye reestaran?*
16 *Soop ocheen' fkoosniy.*
17 *K sazhilyeneeyu doosh nye rabotaeet.*
18 *Mozhna eetee v reestaran?*
19 *On/ana nee yes't' riboo.*
20 *Soobota nam gadeetsa.*

LET'S SPEAK MORE RUSSIAN

◀) CD2, TR 11

For these optional exercises add an extra 15 minutes to your daily schedule. And remember: near enough is good enough!

IN YOUR OWN WORDS

This exercise will teach you to express yourself freely. Use only the words you have learned so far.

Tell me in your own words that...

1 Mr Ivanov rang you
2 he is a good client of your firm
3 you are going to a restaurant with him on Saturday evening
4 it is possible to meet next week
5 Kate can't go, she has important business
6 Tom has a cold, we must call a doctor
7 you will take steak, fish with potato, a small piece of chicken and salad, tea and cake, please

Ask:

8 Do you have any specials today?
9 Have you known him long?
10 What do you want to drink?

....

Answers

1 *Mnye pazvaneel gaspadeen Eevanof.*
2 *On kharoshiiy kleeyent nashiiy feermi.*
3 *F soobotoo vyecheeram mi s neem eedyom v reestaran.*
4 *Vazmozhno vstryeteetsa na slyedooshshyeeiy needyelee.*
5 *Kate nye mozhit eetee, oo neeyo vazhnaie deela.*

6 *Oo Toma prastooda, nada vizvat' vrachya.*
7 *Mnye, pazhaloosta beefshteks/riboo s kartoshkaiy/koosocheek kooritsi ee salat/chyaiy ee tort.*
8 *Oo vas yes't' seevodnya feermeeniee blyuda?*
9 *Vi yeevo davno znaeetee?*
10 *Shto vi khateetee peet'?*

LET'S SPEAK RUSSIAN – FAST AND FLUENTLY

Translate each section and check if it is correct. Then cover the answers and say the three or four sentences fast!

Can you say each section in 25 seconds?
Some of the English is in 'Russian-speak' to help you.

Today called Boris.
He is our client, very good man.
He in Moscow for two days. By his important meeting.

Seevodnya pazvaneel Barees.
On nash kleeyent, ocheen' kharoshiiy cheelavyek.
On v Maskvye na dva dnya. Oo neevo vazhnaye fstryechya.

What shall we do tomorrow?
In centre, behind church is new restaurant.
By you have time?

Shto mi dyelaeem zaftra?
F tsentree, za tserkvayu yes't' noviy reestaran.
Oo vas yes't' vryemya?

I can't. By me ill wife, necessary it will be to call doctor.
I understand, it's a pity, but on next week?

Ya nee magoo. Oo meenya bal'na zhina, nada boodeet vizvat'
vrachya.
Ya panimayu, ocheen' zhal', a na slyedooshsheeiy needyelee?

Now say all the sentences in Russian without stopping and starting. If you can do it in under 90 seconds you are a fast and fluent winner! But if you are not happy with your result – just try once more!

TEST YOUR PROGRESS

Translate the following sentences in writing. Then check the answers.

1 I think the appointment is on Tuesday.
2 Today? No, I am sorry, that is not possible.
3 I must buy many presents.
4 Can('t) you help me, please? I want the number of the doctor.
5 Do(n't) you know where there is a good restaurant?
6 The church is very interesting, it seems.
7 We would like to travel on Monday evening, please.
8 Can I have the menu, please?
9 Excuse me, please, where are the papers?
10 Can one buy fruit here?
11 Do you know his new restaurant?
12 It was wonderful! Thank you very much for the pleasant evening.
13 Why is it necessary for you to see my credit card?
14 It was boring at the theatre on Monday.
15 You see the telephone upstairs by the exit, by the door.
16 We eat chicken or sausage... the fish is too expensive.
17 How does one say in Russian...?
18 Do(n't) you know where here bus? (where there is a bus here?)
19 My husband wants to go to Texas, but I would like to go to New York.
20 He does not know that the new restaurant is behind the church.

How did you get on? Another brilliant score on the **Progress chart**?

5

Week five

DAY-BY-DAY GUIDE

How about 15 minutes on the train, tube or bus, 10 minutes on the way home and 30 minutes before switching on the television...?

DAY ONE

▶ Read **On their way**.
▶ Listen to/Read **F pootee**.
▶ Read the **New words**. Learn 15 or more.

DAY TWO

▶ Repeat the dialogue. Learn the harder **New words**.
▶ Cut out the **Flash words** to get stuck in.

DAY THREE

▶ Test yourself to perfection on all the **New words**.
▶ Read and learn the **Good news grammar**.

DAY FOUR (THE TOUGH DAY)

▶ Listen to/Read **Learn by heart**.
▶ Cut out and learn the ten **Flash sentences**.

DAY FIVE

▶ Listen to/Read **Spot the keys**.
▶ Go over **Learn by heart**.

DAY SIX

▶ Listen to/Read **Let's speak Russian**.
▶ Listen to/Read **Let's speak more Russian** (optional).
▶ Listen to/Read **Let's speak Russian – fast and fluently** (optional).
▶ Translate **Test your progress**.

DAY SEVEN

I bet you don't want a day off... but I insist!

ON THEIR WAY

Tom and Kate are travelling across Russia by train, bus and taxi. They talk to Olga, the ticket clerk, to Jim in the train and to Tatyana in the bus.

(At the station...)

Tom   Two tickets to Tver, please.

Olga   There and back?

Tom   There and how (what)? More slowly, please.

Olga   There... and... back.

Tom   To one end (single) only, please. When leaves train and from where?

Olga   At 9.45, from fifth platform.

Kate   More quickly (hurry), Tom, here are two places, for non- smokers. Oh, here is someone here smoking. Excuse me, in the train not possible to smoke. Because these seats are for non-smokers. Here to smoke is forbidden.

Jim   Sorry, I don't understand. I speak only English.

(At the bus stop...)

Kate   On Sundays few buses. For us it is necessary to wait 20 minutes. Tom, here are my postcards and letter. Over there post box. And I want to take couple of photographs. River so beautiful in sun.

Tom   Kate, hurry. Are arriving two buses. Both yellow. First already full, the other is better.

(In the bus...)

Tatyana Tickets it is necessary to punch!

Tom   Oh, yes, thank you. To museum it is far?

Tatyana This bus goes not to museum, but to hospital.

(In the taxi...)

Tom   I very pleased. Taxi not bad and journey not too expensive costs.

Kate   To me does not please this car (I don't like), because it old and not clean... that's why cheaper. I hope that problems will not be.

F POOTEE

Tom and Kate are travelling across Russia by train, bus and taxi.
They talk to Olga, the ticket clerk, to Jim in the train and to
Tatyana in the bus.

(Na vagzalee...)

Tom	Dva beel**ye**ta f Tvyer, pazh**a**loosta.
Olga	Tood**a** ee abr**a**tna?
Tom	Tood**a** ee kak? Pam**ye**dleeneeye, pazh**a**loosta.
Olga	Tood**a**... ee... abr**a**tna.
Tom	Tol'ka, v ad**ee**n kan**ye**ts pazh**a**loosta. Kagd**a** atkh**o**deet p**o**eest ee atk**oo**da?
Olga	V d**ye**veet' s**o**rak pyat', ot p**ya**taiy platf**o**rmi.
Kate	Skar**ye**ye, Tom, vot dva myest**a**, dlya neekoor**ya**shsheekh. Akh, vot kto-ta z'dyes' k**oo**reet'. Eezveen**ee**tee, f p**o**eezdee neel'zya koor**ee**t'. Patam**oo** shta **e**tee meest**a** dlya neekoor**ya**shsheekh. Z'dyes' koor**ee**t' zapreesh**a**eetsa.
Jim	Sorry, I don't understand. Ya gavar**yu** only English.

*(Na astan**o**fkee aft**o**boosa...)*

Kate	Pa vaskrees**ye**n'yam m**a**la aft**o**boosaf. Nam n**a**da zhdat' dv**a**tsat meen**oo**t. Tom, vot ma**ee** atr**ki**tkee ee pees'm**o**. Von tam pacht**o**viy **ya**shsheek. A ya khach**oo** s'nyat' p**a**roo fatagr**a**feeiy. Reek**a** tak kras**ee**va na s**o**ntsi.
Tom	Kate, skar**ye**ye! Vot dva aft**o**boosa. **O**ba zh**o**ltiee. P**ye**rvyiy **oo**zhe p**o**lan, droog**o**iy l**oo**chshi.

*(F avt**o**boosee...)*

Tatyana	Beel**ye**ti n**a**da prakampas't**ee**ravat'!
Tom	Akh, da, kan**ye**shna. Do mooz**ye**ya dal**ee**ko?
Tatyana	**E**tat aft**o**boos **ye**deet nye v mooz**ye**iy, a v bal'n**ee**tsoo.

*(F taks**ee**...)*

Tom	Ya **o**cheen' dav**o**leen. Taks**ee** neeplakh**o**ye ee pa**ye**stka nye sl**ee**shkam d**o**raga st**o**eet.
Kate	Mnye nye nr**a**veetsa **e**ta mash**i**na, patam**oo** shta st**a**raya ee nyech**ee**staya, vot pacheem**oo** deesh**e**vlee. Ya nad**ye**yus', shto prabl**ye**m nye b**oo**deet.

Tom	There was only this taxi. *(Later...)* Where we? I don't see museum. On left petrol station and station of metro. On right school.
Kate	Here is plan of town. To museum, it seems, it is not far... to traffic lights, then right along main street. Why we so slowly travelling? Petrol has finished? Oil has finished? Taxi has broken down? Where my bag? Where mobile phone?
Tom	Kate, these questions lead me from mind (are driving me crazy). And it is raining. And why police travelling behind us?

NEW WORDS

🔊 **CD2, TR 14**

poot'/pootee *way, journey*

vagzal *(railway) station*

beelyet/beelyety *ticket/tickets*

dva beelyeta *two tickets*

tooda *to there*

abratna *back/return*

pamyedleeneeye *a little more slowly*

kanyets *end, direction (one way)*

atkhadeet'/atkhodeet *to leave/it leaves*

poeest/f poeezdee *train/in the train*

atkooda *from where*

platforma/platformi *platform*

skaryeye *hurry*

neekooryashsheekh *non-smokers*

kooreet' *to smoke*

patamoo shta *because*

zapreeshshaeetsa *it is forbidden*

astanofka *bus stop*

pa vaskreesyeneeyam *on Sundays*

mala *few, little*

zhdat' *to wait*

pees'mo *letter*

von tam *over there*

pachtoviy yashsheek *post box*

snyat' *to take (of photographs)*

para/paroo *pair, couple*

fatagrafiya/fatagrafeeiy *photograph/photographs*

reeka *river*

sontse *sun*

oba *both*

pyervyiy *first*

polan *full*

Tom	Bila tol'ka eta tak**see**. *(Pozhe...)* Gdye mi? Ya nee ve**e**zhoo mooz**yeiy**. Nal**ye**va benzazapr**a**fka ee st**a**ntseeya meetr**o**. Napr**a**va shk**o**la.
Kate	Vot plan g**o**rada. Da mooz**ye**ya, k**a**zhitsa, needaleek**o**... da sveetaf**o**ra, pat**o**m napr**a**va po gl**a**vnaiy **oo**leetsi. Pacheem**oo** mi tak m**ye**dleena **ye**deem? Beenz**ee**n konch**ee**ls'a? M**a**sla konch**ee**las'? Taks**ee** slam**a**las? Gdye ma**ya soo**mka? Gdye s**o**taviy teel**ee**f**o**n?
Tom	Kate, **e**tee vapr**o**see sv**o**dyat meen**ya** s oom**a**. Ee eed**yo**t dosht'. A pacheem**oo** meel**ee**tsiya **ye**deet za nam**ee**?

droog**oiy** *other, another*	beenzazapr**a**fka *petrol station*
prakampast**ee**ravat' *to punch, clip*	*(colloquial)*
mooz**yeiy**/mooz**ye**ya *museum*	st**a**ntseeya meetr**o**
(nee) daleek**o** *it is (not) far,*	*metro station*
(not) distant	shk**o**la *school*
et**at**/**e**ta *this*	plan g**o**rada *plan of the town*
bal'n**ee**tsa/bal'n**ee**tsoo	sveetaf**o**r/sveetaf**o**ra *traffic*
hospital	*lights*
neeplakh**o**ye *not bad*	gl**a**vnaiy **oo**leetsi *main street*
pay**e**stka *journey*	m**ye**dleena *slowly*
m**a**shina *car*	beenz**ee**n *petrol*
st**a**roye/st**a**raya *old*	konch**ee**lsa/k**o**nch**ee**las' *has*
neech**ee**staya *not clean*	*finished*
nad**ye**yatsa/nad**ye**yus' *to hope/*	m**a**sla *oil*
I hope	slam**a**las' *it has broken down*
taks**ee** *taxi*	sv**o**dyat meen**ya** s oom**a** *are*
eed**yo**t dosht' *it's raining*	*driving me crazy*
v**ee**deet'/v**ee**zhoo *to see/ I see*	meel**ee**tsiya *police*

TOTAL NEW WORDS: 60
...only 38 words to go!

LEARN BY HEART

Someone crashed the car and someone else is getting suspicious!

Mashina tol'ka neemnoshka slamalas...

Zaftra nam mozhna smatryet' tenees? Oo meenya dva beelyeta
na mach. Ya khachu veedeet' novykh ameereekanskeekh
tineeseestaf.* Mozhna yekhat' tooda na meetro? Eelee loochshe
na aftoboosee, patamoo shta on yedeet pryama na stadeeon.

Aftoboos? Meetro? Pacheemoo? Mnye nye nraveetsa garatskoiy
transport. Oo nas kraseevaya mashina.

Da, no... vcheera, kagda ya yekhala v gorat, ya nee ooveedeela
sveetafor... no mashina tol'ka nyemnoshka slamalas...

*tineeseestaf: tennis players

GOOD NEWS GRAMMAR

◀) CD2, TR 16

1 NRAVEETSA – *TO LIKE – OR NOT LIKE*

Think how often you use this in English: *I like this – you don't
like that – do you like...?*

In Russian you use **nraveetsa**, but it is a bit of a strange
construction. Think of it as *something that is pleasing to you*:

I like the car – *To me is pleasing the car.*	**Mnye nraveetsa mashina.**
We don't like the car – *To us is not pleasing the car.*	**Nam nye nraveetsa mashina.**
Do you like to work? – *To you is pleasing to work?*	**Vam nraveetsa rabotat'?**

Once you get used to is pleasing it's quite simple really. Just remember **nraveetsa**.

2 SAYING THE OPPOSITE – JUST ADD NEE

This an easy way to double your vocabulary! As opposed to learning two words just use one and add 'nee':

Eta kraseeviy gorat.	*It is a beautiful town.*
Eta neekraseeviy gorat.	*It is an ugly (not beautiful) town.*
Magzeenee neeinteryesnyee.	*The shops are boring (not interesting).*

3 ANOTHER SHORTCUT – 'CAN' AND 'CAN'T'

In such common phrases as *Can you hear…?* or *Can't you see…?* the Russians will leave out the *can* or *can't* altogether:

Ya slishoo yeevo.	*I can hear him.*
Vi nye veedeetee teeleeveezar?	*Can't you see the television?*

Makes it easier, doesn't it?

4 NO MORE NEW GRAMMAR!

After this week there's no more new grammar. After all, you decided on **Fast-track Russian** because you wanted a starter kit – not a complicated textbook.

If you remember all the grammar notes, words and phrases in the book you'll have done very well indeed.

LET'S SPEAK RUSSIAN

◀) CD2, TR 17

A ten-point warm-up: I give you an answer and you ask me a question as if you did not hear the words in CAPITAL LETTERS very well.

Example: Veektar Z'DYES'. *Question* Gdye Veektar?

1 Sotaviy teeleefon V SOOMKEE.
2 SHKOLA von tam.
3 Poeest atkhodeet V TREE CHEESA.
4 TOM khocheet gavareet' s Bareesam Eevanaveecheem.
5 Beelyet tooda ee abratna stoeet 80 ROOBLYEIY.
6 Mnye nye nraveetsa mashina, PATAMOO SHTA ana staraya.
7 Vi yedeetee v Angleeyu ... NA SAMALYOTEE.
8 Ya ooveedeel(a) SVEETAFOR.
9 DA, mnye nraveetsa gasteeneetsa.
10 Mnye nraveetsa MOOZYEIY.

Now answer starting with 'da':

11 Vi znaeetee noviy magazeen?
12 Vam nraveetsa reeka?
13 Vi veedeetee astanofkoo aftoboosa?

Here are three things that you want to refer to. But you don't know what they are called in Russian. Explain them using the words you know:

14 a refrigerator
15 a holiday
16 a kennel

Answers

1 *Gdye sotavyiy teeleefon?*
2 *Shto eta von tam?*
3 *Kagda atkhodeet poeest?*
4 *Kto khocheet gavereet' s Bareesam Eevanaveecheem?*
5 *Skol'ka stoeet beelyet tooda ee abratna?*
6 *Pacheemoo vam nye nraveetsa mashina?*
7 *Kak vi yedeete v Angleeyu?*
8 *Shto vi ooveedeelee?*
9 *Vam nraveetsa gasteeneetsa?*
10 *Shto vam nraveetsa?*
11 *Da, ya znayu noviy magazeen.*
12 *Da, mnye nraveetsa reeka.*
13 *Da, ya veezhoo astanofkoo aftoboosa.*
14 *Meesta, gdye kholadna, dlya malaka, myasa, sira.*
15 *Vryemya, kagda vi nye rabotaeetee.*
16 *Dom dlya sabakee, kagda mi v otpooskee.*

LET'S SPEAK MORE RUSSIAN

◀) CD2, TR 18

IN YOUR OWN WORDS

This exercise will teach you to express yourself freely. Use only the words you have learned so far.

Tell me in your own words that...

1 the train leaves at 10.30 from the first platform
2 you hope there won't be any problems
3 on Saturdays there are few buses; it is necessary to wait for a long time
4 it is necessary to punch the tickets
5 the taxi is not expensive, but the car is old

6 you need two tickets to St Petersburg, there and back

7 you want to take a couple of photos, the church is
so beautiful

8 you are driving along the main street to the railway station,
then to the right

9 you can't see the taxi

Ask:

10 where are seats for non-smokers?

....

Answers

1 *Poeesd atkhodeet v
dyeseet' treetsat ot pyervaiy
platformi.*

2 *Ya nadyeyus', shto prablyem
nye boodeet.*

3 *Pa soobotam mala
aftoboosaf, nada dolgo
zhdat'.*

4 *Nada prakampasteeravat'
beelyety.*

5 *Taksee stoeet nyedoraga, no
mashina staraya.*

6 *Mnye dva beelyeta f Sankt-
Peeteerboork, tooda i abratna.*

7 *Ya khachu snyat' paroo
fatagrafeeiy, tserkaf tak
kraseevaya.*

8 *Mi yedeem po glavnaiy
ooleetsi do vagzala, patom
naprava.*

9 *Ya nee veezhoo taksee.*

10 *Gdye meesta dlya
neekooryashsheekh?*

LET'S SPEAK RUSSIAN – FAST AND FLUENTLY

◀) CD2, TR 19

Translate each section and check if it is correct. Then cover the answers and say the three or four sentences as quickly as you can. Try to say each section in less than 30 seconds.

Ticket one way to Tver. How much?
More slowly, please. Yes, for me on train at 11.30.
Where platform number 5?

Beelyet v adeen kanyets f Tvyer'. Skol'ka?
Pamyedleeneeye, pazhaloosta. Da, mnye na poeest v adinatsat tritsat.
Gdye platforma nomeer pyat?

We need the post box.
Here are letter and photo.
More quickly, the bus is full again.
Other one it necessary to wait ten minutes.

Nam noozhin pachtoviy yashsheek.
Vot pees'mo ee fatagrafiya.
Skaryeye, aftoboos apyat' polan.
Droogoiy nada zhdat' dyeseet' meenoot.

Ten minutes wait, let's go on taxi.
To the metro, it seems, not far.
Along the main street, to the traffic light, then to the left.
Where my mobile phone?

Dyeseet' minoot zhdat', yedeem na taksee.
Do meetro, kazhitsa, nyedaleeko.
Po glavnaiy ooleetsi, do sveetafora, patom nalyeva.
Gdye moiy sotaviy teeleefon?

Now say all the sentences in Russian without stopping and starting. If you can do it in under 90 seconds you are a fast and fluent winner!

But if you are not happy with your result – just try once more!

SPOT THE KEYS

◆) CD2, TR 20

This time you are planning a trip in the country and want to have some idea what the weather will be like. This is what you could ask:

You	Eezveeneetee, pazhaloosta, vi nye mozhitee mnye skazat', kakaya zaftra boodeet pagoda?
Answer	*Eezveeneetee, ya nee znayu, no kagdayasmatryel* pragnoz pagodi po teeleeveezaroo, *skazalee, shto* pagoda myedleena *meenyaeetsa*. Zaftra *boodeet kholadna* – voseem' gradoosaf, s *neebal'shimvyetram ee* dosht boodeet k vyecheeroo.

She doesn't know, but according to the TV something slow is happening and it will be cold tomorrow, 8°C, with rain in the evening.

TEST YOUR PROGRESS

1 I don't like this bag. The other bag was better.
2 How much does (the) ticket cost – return?
3 What did you say? Slowly, please.
4 I know that in America petrol is cheaper.
5 In (the) underground it is forbidden to smoke.
6 I cannot wait, I have (an) appointment at 11 o'clock.
7 Is this (the) letter box? (A) yellow letter box?
8 Hello, we are 30 km from Novgorod. Is that (the) petrol station?
9 Which is cheaper? (The) bus or (the) metro?
10 Today it is very cold. I hope that it will rain.
11 The traffic light was red, not green. That's why they're both in hospital.
12 She was at (the) petrol station on Monday and Tuesday. The car drinks petrol!
13 Where here (is the) dry cleaner's? By me oil on T-shirt 'Armani'.
14 Our flat (is) behind (the) main street, by (the) bus stop.
15 We are by police (at the police station), because we do not know where my mobile phone (is).
16 It is necessary to buy (the) tickets now, because they cheaper.
17 I like your car. Was it very expensive?
18 Can you help us, please? Can one eat here by river?

If you know all your words you should score over 90%!

6

Week six

DAY-BY-DAY GUIDE

This is your last week! Need I say more?

DAY ONE

▶ Read **In the airport**.
▶ Listen to/Read **V aerapartoo**.
▶ Read the **New words**. There are only a handful!

DAY TWO

▶ Read **V aerapartoo**. Learn all the **New words**.
▶ Work with the **Flash words** and **Flash sentences**.

DAY THREE

▶ Test yourself on the **Flash sentences**.
▶ No more **Good news grammar**! Try the quiz instead.

DAY FOUR

▶ Listen to/Read and learn **Da sveedaneeya**.
▶ Listen to/Read **Spot the keys**.

DAY FIVE

▶ Listen to/Read **Let's speak Russian**.
▶ Read **Say it simply**.

DAY SIX

▶ Listen to/Read **Let's speak more Russian** (optional).
▶ Listen to/Read **Let's speak Russian – fast and fluently** (optional).
▶ Your last **Test your progress**! Go for it!

DAY SEVEN

Congratulations!
You have successfully completed the course
and can now speak

Fast-track Russian!

IN THE AIRPORT

Tom and Kate are on their way back to Birmingham. They are in the departure lounge at Moscow airport.

Tom	On Monday for us it is necessary will be to work. Terrible! I want (to go) to Italy or to Hawaii! No one in my firm knows where I (am).
Kate	And in my firm? They know (the) number of telephone of my mother, and she knows the number of my mobile telephone…
Tom	Yes, yes, I know. Well, perhaps at Christmas, (a) week in the snow or let's go on (a) ship to Madeira. But I want to buy (a) newspaper downstairs… Kate! There is Yuriy Zhivago!
Yuriy	Hello! How are things? What you here are doing? This is my wife, Nancy. Already (the) end of your holiday? Well, how all went? (How did it go?)
Kate	Splendidly! (wonderful). We much saw and too much ate. Now we well know Moscow, and Saint Petersburg…
Yuriy	Next year for you it is necessary to (go to) Novgorod! Mrs Walker, my wife wants to buy a book for our computer. You (not) can help her (Could you help her at all?) Mr Walker, you have a newspaper. Give, please, (the) Sport. Then I invite you to (the) bar.
(At the airport kiosk…)	
Kate	Here nothing suitable there is [not]. You also going to England?
Nancy	No, we are going to Saint Petersburg. Mother of Yuriy lives there. Our children were by her for two weeks. By us (we have) boy and three girls. Tomorrow we are going to Novgorod on the train. It is cheaper.
Kate	Your husband works in (a) bank?

V AERAPARTOO

Tom and Kate are on their way back to Birmingham. They are in the departure lounge of Moscow airport.

Tom	F paneed**ye**lneek n**a**m nada b**oo**deet rabotat'. **Oo**zhas! Ya khach**u** v It**a**leeyu **ee**lee na Gav**ai**yee! Neekt**o** v ma**yeiy** f**ee**rmee nye zn**a**eet, gdye ya.
Kate	A v ma**yeiy** f**ee**rmee? An**ee** zn**a**yut n**o**meer teeleef**o**na ma**yeiy** m**a**mi, a an**a** zn**a**eet n**o**meer mayev**o** s**o**tavava teeleef**o**na.
Tom	Da, da, zn**a**yu. Noo, m**o**zhit bit' na Razhdeestv**o**, need**ye**lyu f snyeg**oo** **ee**lee pa**ye**deem na teeplakh**o**dee na Mad**yeiy**roo. A ya khach**u** koop**eet**' gaz**ye**too vneez**oo**... Kate! Vot **Yu**riy Zhiv**a**ga!
Yuriy	Zdr**a**stvooiytee! Kak deel**a**? Shto vi z'dyes' d**ye**laeetee? **E**ta m**a**ya zhin**a**, Nancy. Oozh**e** kan**ye**ts v**a**shiva **o**tpooska? Noo, kak fsyo prashl**o**?
Kate	Veeleekal**ye**pna! Mi mn**o**ga v**ee**deelee ee sl**ee**shkam mn**o**ga **ye**lee. Seech**ya**s mi kharash**o** zn**a**eem ee Maskv**oo** ee Sankt-Peeteerb**oo**rk...
Yuriy	F sl**ye**dooshsheem gad**oo** vam n**a**da v N**o**vgarat! Gaspazh**a** Walker, m**a**ya zhin**a** kh**o**cheet koop**eet**' kn**ee**goo dlya n**a**shiva kamp'**yu**tira. Vi nye m**o**zhitee yeiy pam**o**ch'? Gaspad**ee**n Walker, oo vas gaz**ye**ta. D**ai**ytee, pazh**a**loosta, *Sport*. Pat**o**m preeglash**a**yu vas v bar.
*(V aerapart**oo**, ookee**o**ska...)*	
Kate	Z'dyes' neecheev**o** patkhad**ya**shsheeva nyet. Vi t**o**zhe **ye**deetee v **A**ngleeyu?
Nancy	Nyet, mi **ye**deem f Sankt-Peeteerb**oo**rk. M**a**ma **Yu**riiya zhiv**yo**t tam. N**a**shi d**ye**tee b**i**lee oo nee**yo** dvye need**ye**lee. Oo nas m**a**l'cheek ee tree d**ye**vachkee. Z**a**ftra mi **ye**deem v N**o**vgarat na p**o**eezdee. **E**ta deeesh**e**vlee.
Kate	Vash moosh rab**o**taeet v b**a**nkee?

Nancy	Yes, his work (is) interesting, but money (is) not big. To our Lada already nine years (our Lada is already nine years old) and by us (we have) old, small flat. (In) this year much (we) have repaired. My parents and my girlfriend (are) in (the) USA and we often write letters. I would like (to go) to America, but too expensive costs.
Kate	But by you (you have) (a) beautiful house in Greece.
Nancy	(A) house in Greece? I never [not] was in Greece (I have never been to Greece). When by us (we have) (a) holiday, we go to friend('s), at Chee**lya**beensk.
Tom	Kate, hurry, for us it is time (to go). What said Mrs Zhivago?
Kate	Wait, Tom, wait!

NEW WORDS

🔊 **CD2, TR 22**

Italeeya/v Ita**lee**yu *Italy/to Italy*
Ga**vai**yee *Hawaii*
mami/**ma**ma *mother*
Razh**dees**tvo *Christmas*
snyek/snee**goo** *snow*
pay**e**deem *let's go*
teepla**khot**/teepla**kho**dee *ship*
Ma**dyeiy**ra/Ma**dyeiy**roo *Madeira*
vnee**zoo** *downstairs*
kak **dee**la? *how are things?*
prashlo *it went by, passed*
veelee**kal**yepna *splendid(ly), great, wonderful(ly)*
yelee *we/they ate*
f s**lye**dooshshee/**e**tam gadoo *next/this year*
k**nee**ga *book*

daiytee *give!*
preegla**shat**'/preegla**sha**yu *to invite/I invite*
bar *bar*
nee**chee**vo *nothing*
patkha**dya**shsheeiy/ patkha**dya**shsheeva *suitable*
zhiv**yot** *lives*
dyetee *children*
dvye (f) *two*
mal'cheek *boy*
dyevachka/**dye**vachkee *(little) girl/girls*
deesh**yev**lee *cheaper*
moosh *husband*
Lada/**La**doo *Lada*
lyet *of years*
ma**leen**'keeiy/ma**leen**'kaya *small*

92

Nancy	Da, yeevo rabota eenteeryesnaya, no dyen'gee nyebal'shiee. Nasheeiy Ladee oozhe dyeveet' lyet ee oo nas staraya, maleen'kaya kvarteera. V etam gadoo mnoga atreemanteeravalee. Maee radeeteelee ee padrooga f S-SHA ee mi chyasta peeshim pees'ma. Ya ocheen' khatyela bi v Amyereekoo, no sleeshkam doraga stoeet.
Kate	No oo vas kraseevyiy dom v Gryetsi-ee.
Nancy	Dom v Gryetsi-ee? Ya neekagda nee bila v Gryetsi-ee. Kagda oo nas otpoosk, mi yedeem k droogoo f Cheelyabeensk.
Tom	Kate! Skaryeye, nam para! Shto skazala gaspazha Zhivaga?
Kate	Padazhdee, Tom, padazhdee!

S-SHA *USA*

peeshim *we write*

chyasta *often*

pees'ma *letters*

neekagda nee *never*

droog/droogoo *friend*

para *it is time (to go)*

padazhdee! *wait!*

TOTAL NEW WORDS: 38

Total Russian words learned: 381
Extra words: 80

GRAND TOTAL: 461

LEARN BY HEART

This is your last dialogue to **Learn by heart**. Give it your best!
You now have six prize-winning party pieces, and a large store
of everyday sayings which will be very useful.

Da sveedaneeya!

Kate Barees Vadeemaveech, gavareet Kate Walker, a ya
v aerapartoo v Maskvye. Da, oozhe kanyets nashiva
otpooska ee nasheekh dyeneek tozhe! Spaseeba
balshoye za ocheen' preeyatniiy vyecheer! Tom
khocheet gavareet' s vamee.

Tom Zdrastvooiytee, Barees Vadeemaveech... Kak? Vi
khateetee koopeet'oba? Oo mayeiy feermi yes't'
vash e-mail? Veeleekalyepna. Spaseeba balshoye!
F slyedooshsheem gadoo?... Kate khocheet v Italeeyu,
no mnye nraveetsa Raseeya.* S Edith Palmer? Akh, Bozhe
moiy, nyet, nyet! Nash samalyot zhdyot**... Noo...
Da sveedaneeya!

*Raseeya: *Russia*
**zhdyot: *is waiting*

GOOD NEWS GRAMMAR

There's no more grammar this week, just a couple of interesting points.

1 DOUBLE NEGATIVE

The Russians love to say nyet so they sometimes say it twice!

Neekto nye znaeet, gdye ya.	*No one not knows where I am.*
Ya neekagda nye bila v Gryetsi-ee.	*I never not was in Greece.*

2 SURNAMES

Yuriy Baranav... and his wife, Mrs Baranava. In Russian, a man's surname usually ends in a consonant and a woman's in the letter 'a' (thus Anna Karyeneena's husband's surname was Karyeneen).

3 QUIZ

And now for some light relief: the end of course quiz!

No marks for this one – just a pat on the back!

1 In which city would you find the Kryeml'?
- **a** Sankt-Peeteerboork
- **b** Maskva
- **c** Yalta
- **d** Vladeevastok

2 How would you say 12 o'clock in Russian?
- **a** dva cheesa
- **b** dvatsat' cheesof
- **c** dveenatsat' cheesof

3 How would you greet someone if you met them in the evening?
- **a** dobraye ootra
- **b** dobriiy dyen'
- **c** da sveedaneeya
- **d** dobriiy vyecheer

4 If you were a vegetarian, which of these would you not eat?
- **a** myasa
- **b** frookti
- **c** tort
- **d** kartoshka

5 When do you celebrate Christmas in Russia?
- **a** 24 deekabrya
- **b** 25 deekabrya
- **c** 31 deekabrya
- **d** 6 yeenvarya

6 If you wanted to apologize, what would you say?
- **a** kharasho
- **b** eezveeneetee
- **c** oozhasna
- **d** kanyeshna

7 When does **Dyet Maros** (the Russian version of Father Christmas) bring presents?
- **a** 24 deekabrya
- **b** 25 deekabrya
- **c** 31 deekabrya
- **d** 6 yeenvarya

8 What does **shto vam** mean?
- **a** Where are you?
- **b** What would you like?
- **c** Where do you work?

9 How do you say in Russian *I understand*?
- **a** ya paneemayu
- **b** ya znayu
- **c** ya khachu
- **d** ya magoo

10 What do Russians say when they really don't approve of what you want to do?
- **a** tak mozhna
- **b** tak neel'zya
- **c** tak nada
- **d** tak nye gadeetsa

You'll find the answers in the **Answers** section.

SPOT THE KEYS

🔊 **CD2, TR 24**

Here's a final practice round. If you have the recording, close the book now. Find the key words and try to get the gist of it. Then check your answers.

This is what you might ask a taxi driver:

You   Skol'ka meenoot do aeraporta ee skol'ka stoeet?

Answer *Eta zaveeseet ot tavo, kagda vi yedeetee. Abichna
payestka dleetsa dvatsat' meenoot, no yeslee vi
khateetee yekhat' f chyasee peek ee veez'dee propkee,
payestka mozhit dleetsa sorak pyat ... asobeenna pa
pyatneetsam, kagda khoozhe fseevo. Skol'ka stoeet?
Abichna ot treetsatee do peeteedeeseetee rooblyeiy.*

SAY IT SIMPLY

1 You are staying in a hotel in Russia. The television and the shower are both broken. Report it – you want to use both!

2 You are at the airport, about to catch your flight home when you realize that you have left a bag behind in the room of your hotel. You phone the hotel reception and ask for it to be sent on to you.

What would you say in these two cases? Say it then write it down. Then see the two examples in the **Answers** section. Yours can be different and even simpler, based solely on your **fast-track** vocabulary. Give it a go!

LET'S SPEAK RUSSIAN

◄ CD2, TR 25

Here's a quick warm-up. Answer the questions using the words in brackets.

1 On koopeel dom v Marbella? (da, paneedyel'neek)
2 Skol'ka lyet vi rabotalee v bankee? (pyat)
3 Kagda vi gavareelee s vashiiy feermaiy? (fcheera)
4 Pacheemoo vam nada atryemanteeravat' vashoo mashinoo? (patamoo shta, ana staraya)
5 On bil snachala v gasteeneetsi? (nyet, f kvarteeree)

Now practise your verbs with **nada, neelzya** and **para**:

6 Oozhas! Kvarteera ocheen' staraya... (You mustn't buy it.)
7 Skaryeye! Oozhe dyeveet' cheesof... (It's time for us to go.)
8 ... (You must mend the television), yeslee on nee rabotaeet.

Finish off the sentences, using phrases which start with **shto** and **patamoo shta**:

9 Maya padrooga skazala... (that already end of holiday).
10 Eeshshyo ana skazala... (that she really likes Moscow).
11 Maya zhina khocheet skazat'... (that she has (a) cold).
12 Moiy moosh gavareet, shto on nee mozhit f tyatr... (because he is working).
13 Ol'ga tozhe ne mozhit f tyatr... (because she is on holiday).
14 Moiy droog gavareet... (that she is very beautiful).
15 On gavareet tozhe... (that he wants her telephone number).

Answers

1 *Da, on koopeel dom v Marbella f paneedyel'neek.*

2 *Ya rabotal/rabotala v bankee pyat lyet.*

3 *Ya gavareel/gavareela s mayeiy feermaiy fcheera.*

4 *Nam nada atreemanteeravat' mashinoo, patamoo shta ana staraya.*

5 *Nyet, snachala on bil f kvarteeree.*

6 *Oozhas! Kvarteera ocheen' staraya. Vam nee nada yeyo.*

7 *Skaryeye! Oozhe dyeveet cheesof. Nam para eetee.*

8 *Vam nada atreemanteeravat' teeleeveezar, yeslee on nee rabotaeet.*

9 *Maya padrooga skazala, shto oozhe kanyets otpooska.*

10 *Eeshshyo ana skazala, shto yeiy ocheen' nraveetsa Maskva.*

11 *Maya zhina khoch'eet skazat', shto oo neeyo prastooda.*

12 *Moiy moosh gavareet, shto on nee mozhit v tyatr, patamoo shta on rabotayet.*

13 *Ol'ga tozhe ne mozhit f tyatr, patamoo shta ana v otpooskye.*

14 *Moiy droog gavareet, shto ana ocheen' kraseevaya.*

15 *On gavareet tozhe, shto on khocheet yeeyo nomeer teeleefona.*

LET'S SPEAK MORE RUSSIAN

◄) CD2, TR 26

IN YOUR OWN WORDS

This exercise will teach you to express yourself freely. Use only the words you have learned so far.

Tell me in your own words that...

1 tomorrow is the end of your holiday
2 nobody knows where you have been
3 next year you are going on a ship to Saint-Petersburg
4 your mother knows the number of your mobile phone
5 you are going to Novgorod on the train; it is cheaper
6 now you know Tver well
7 at Christmas you are going to your friend in England
8 his wife works in Moscow
9 your children were with (by) him in the flat
10 you like the restaurant

....

Answers

1 *Zaftra kanyets nashiva otpooska.*

2 *Neekto nye znaeet, gdye mi bilee.*

3 *V slyedooyshsheem gadoo mi payedeem na teeplakhodee f Sankt-Peeteerboork.*

4 *Mama znaeet nomeer nashiva sotavava teeleefona.*

5 *Mi yedeem v Novgarat na poeezdee, tak deeshevlee.*

6 *Seechas mi kharasho znaeem Tvyer.*

7 *Na Razhdeestvo mi payedeem g droogoo v Angleeyu.*

8 *Yeevo zhina rabotaeet v Maskvye.*

9 *Nashi dyetee bilee oo neevo v kvarteeree.*

10 *Mnye nraveetsa reestaran.*

LET'S SPEAK RUSSIAN – FAST AND FLUENTLY

◀ CD2, TR 27

Translate each section and check if it is correct. Then cover the answers and say the sentences as quickly as you can!

I want to (go to) Hawaii for several days.
We have never been in Moscow.
In my firm they know the number of my mobile phone.

Ya khachu na Gavaiyee na nyeskal'ka dnyeiy.
Mi neekagda nye bilee v Maskvye.
V mayeiy feermee znayut nomeer sotavava teelefona.

The girlfriend invites me to Greece on the boat.
It is interesting, but expensive costs. Cheaper to buy ticket to Sochi.
There by us beautiful house.

Padrooga preeglashaeet meenya v Gryetsiyu na teeplakhodee.
Eta eenteeryesna, no doraga stoeet. Deeshevlee koopeet' beelyet
f Sochee.
Tam oo nas kraseeviy dom.

What are you doing here? My husband wants to buy computer.
You can't us help? Here nothing suitable not.
Downstairs can buy cheaper.

Shto vi z'dyes' dyelaeetee? Moiy moosh khocheet koopeet'
kamp'yutir.
Vi nye mozhitee nam pamoch'? Z'dyes' neecheevo
padhadyashsheeva nyet.
Vneezoo mozhna koopeet' deeshevlee.

Now say all the sentences in Russian without stopping and starting.
If you can do it in under 90 seconds you are a fast and fluent winner!

TEST YOUR PROGRESS

A lot of 'fast-track' verbs have been included in this test.. But don't panic – it looks worse than it is. Go for it – you'll do brilliantly.

1 I like writing letters because I have (a) new computer.
2 How are you? You have (a) problem? To help you (Can I help you?).
3 Excuse me, do you have the number of (her) mobile?
4 I like (the) Crimea (Krim). It is never cold there.
5 The other case is in (the) bus. Have you got (the) brown bag?
6 Where will you be at Christmas?
7 Who wants fish and who wants meat?
8 He has my telephone number. He often rings me.
9 Quickly! Where is (the) ticket? The train is coming!
10 Don't you know that (the) airport is always open?
11 My holiday is very important. I want (to go) to Italy.
12 Have you seen Olga in the newspaper? Without (her) husband?
13 Your mother is very pleasant. Her walnut cake is delicious!
14 We must work. We have three boys and one girl. Very expensive costs!
15 Excuse me, where is it possible to repair (the) car?
16 I know him. He always goes shopping with (his) dog.
17 Who said it is impossible (one cannot) here to smoke?
18 We are travelling to (the) airport by taxi, then to Dallas by plane.
19 I would like to speak to (the) waiter. Where is (the) bill?
20 I am sorry, but this is the end of **Fast-track Russian**.

Check your answers, then enter your final excellent score on the **Progress chart** and write out your certificate!

....

Answers

HOW TO SCORE

From a total of 100%

▶ Subtract 1% for each wrong or missing word.
▶ Subtract 1% for the wrong form of the verb, like **yede**em when it should be **yed**oo.
▶ Subtract 1% for mixing up the pronouns such as vi, vam, vamee.

There are no penalties for:

▶ Wrong or different ending of the word, e.g. kamp'yutir – kamp'yutira. In a very few cases you will not already have met the correct word ending that you see in the answer. As long as you have the right word, you're doing fine and will be understood. Remember, near enough is good enough.
▶ Picking the wrong 'version' of the word, e.g. noviy – novim.
▶ Picking the wrong word where there are two of similar meaning, e.g. no and a.
▶ Wrong spelling, as long as you can say the word! e.g. **ee**yun – iy**oo**n.
▶ Different word order.

For each test, correct your mistakes. Then read the corrected answers out loud twice.

> **100% MINUS YOUR PENALTIES WILL GIVE
> YOU YOUR WEEKLY SCORE.**

WEEK 1

TEST YOUR PROGRESS

1 Meenya zavoot Frank Lukas.
2 Zdrastvooitee, mi – Veektar ee Ol'ga.
3 Ya tozhe eez Omska.
4 V aktyabrye ya bil/bila v Maskvye.
5 Mi bilee tree goda v Amyereekee.
6 Londan stoeet doraga.
7 Eezveeneetee, pazhaloosta, gdye vi rabotaeetee?
8 Vi rabotaeete v Manchyes'teeree?
9 Vi Veektar Eezmaiylaf ees Tomska?
10 Kvarteera v Novgaradee ocheen' bal'shaya.
11 Meenootachkoo, pazhaloosta, oo meenya bol'shi dyeneek.
12 Tam yes't' teeleefon? Nyet, k sazhilyeneeyu.
13 Ya v Yaltee bees sina.
14 Feerma bal'shaya?
15 Meerseedes doraga stoeet?
16 V apryelee Londan ocheen' kraseeviiy.
17 Oo neevo f tooragyentstvee padrooga.
18 K sazhilyeneeyu rabota ocheen' skoochnaya.
19 Rabota ocheen' kharoshaya, no otpoosk loochshe.
20 Maya doch vseegda zvaneet.

....
: **YOUR SCORE:** _____% :
....

WEEK 2

TEST YOUR PROGRESS

1 Ya p'yu mnoga shampanskava.
2 Skol'ka stoeet zaftrak, pazhaloosta.
3 Z'dyes' yes't' tooragyenstva?
4 Oo vas yes't' stol? F syem peetnatsat'?

5   Ya khachu peet' kofee.
6   Moiy otpoosk va Flareedee bil loochshe.
7   Gdye kharoshaya gasteeneetsa?
8   Telefoniy shshyot, pazhaloosta.
9   Mi bilee f Sankt-Peeteerboorgee v maee.
10 Moiy dom sleeshkam bal'shoiy.
11 F katoram chyasoo vi v Maskvoo zaftra?
12 Ya tam s vos'mee do peetee.
13 Eezveeneetee, pazhaloosta. Gdye tooalyety, pryama?
14 Mi khateem yekhat' v Osla v yeenvarye, no sleeshkam
    kholadna.
15 Eta stoeet bol'shi dyeneek?
16 Zaftra, gdye vi v dyeseet' treetsat?
17 Oozhasna. Nomeer ocheen' doraga stoeet.
18 Z'dyes' mozhna peet' kofee seechyas? Oo vas yes't' meesta?
19 Oo nas maleenkieeiy dom v Amyereekee, no on ocheen'
    doraga stoeet.
20 Da sveedaneeya, mi yedeem v Yaltoo.

....
: YOUR SCORE: _____%
....

WEEK 3

TEST YOUR PROGRESS

1   Gdye pradavyets?
2   Gdye mozhna koopeet' bootirbrodi?
3   Kagda vam nada v Angleeyu seevodnya? F syem' cheesof?
4   Mi ooveedeelee eta vcheera po teeleeveezaroo.
5   Seechyas magazeeni atkriti, kazhitsa.
6   Z'dyes' yes't' ooneeveermak eelee soopeermarkeet?
7   Eezveeneetee, vi tozhe eedyotee na pochtoo?
8   Gdye vi koopeelee angleeskooyu gazyetoo?
9   Vi khateetye kofee eelee chyaiy?
10 Seevodnya pagoda plakhaya. Neel'zya v Novgarat.
11 Eta fsyo? Eta bila needoraga.

12 Markee stoeelee peetnatsat' roobleiy.

13 Mi preeneemaeem kreedeetniee kartochkee.

14 Treesta gram sira sleeshkam mnoga? Nyet, nyet prablyem.

15 Yes't' novaya kheemcheestka bleeska atsyuda.

16 Oo vas yes't' pakyeteek dlya maeiy foodbolkee, pazhaloosta?

17 Ya z'dyes' ooveedeela aptyekoo, kazhitsa.

18 Bozhe moiy! Aftoboos nee rabotaeet ee Meerseedes tozhe nee rabotaeet!

19 Vi ooveedeelee foodbolkoo? Gdye vi koopeelee yeeyo?

20 Peetsot rooblyeiy, no oo meenya tolka dolari.

WEEK 4

TEST YOUR PROGRESS

1 Ya doomayu, shto fstryechya va ftorneek.

2 Seevodnya? Nyet, eezveeneetee, eta neevazmozhna.

3 Mnye nada koopeet' mnoga padarkaf.

4 Vi nye mozhite mnye pamoch', pazhaloosta? Ya khachu nomeer vrachya.

5 Vi nye znaeete, gdye yes't' kharoshiy reestaran?

6 Tserkaf' ocheen' eentyeryesnaya, kazhitsa.

7 Mi khatyelee bi yekhat' f paneedyel'neek vyecheeram pazhaloosta.

8 Mozhna meenyu, pazhaloosta?

9 Eezveeneetee, pazhaloosta, gdye boomagee?

10 Z'dyes' mozhna koopeet' frookti?

11 Vi znaeete yeevo noviy reestaran?

12 Eta bila preekrasna. Spaseeba balshoye za ocheen' preeyatniy vyecheer.

13 Pacheemoo vam nada veedeet' mayu kreedeetnooyu kartachkoo?

14 Bila skooshna f tyatree f paneedyel'neek.

15 Vi veedeetee teeleefon naveerkhoo, okala vikhada, okala dvyeree.

16 Mi yedeem kooreetsoo eelee kalbasoo... riba sleeshkam doraga stoeet.

17 Kak pa-roosskee...?

18 Vi nee znaeetee, gdye z'dyes' aftoboos?

19 Moiy moosh khocheet yekhat' f Teekhas, a ya khatyela bi yekhat' v N'yu York.

20 On nee znaeet, shto noviy reestaran za tserkav'yu.

WEEK 5

TEST YOUR PROGRESS

1 Mnye nee nraveetsa eta soomka. Droogaya soomka bila loochshe.

2 Skol'ka stoeet beelyet – tooda ee abratna?

3 Shto vi skazalee? Pamyedleeneeye, pazhaloosta.

4 Ya znayu, shto v Amyereekee beenzeen deeshevlee.

5 V meetro kooreet' zapreeshshaeetsa.

6 Ya nye magoo zhdat'. Oo meenya fstryechya v adeenatsat' cheesof.

7 Eta pachtoviy yashsheek? Zholtiy yashsheek?

8 Allo, mi f treetsatee keelamyetrakh ot Novgarada. Eta benzazaprafka?

9 Shto deeshevlee? Aftoboos eelee meetro?

10 Seevodnya ocheen' kholadna. Nadyeyus, boodeet dosht.

11 Sveetafor bil krasnyiy, nee zeelyonyiy. Vot pacheemoo anee oba v balneetsi.

12 Ana bila na benzazaprafkoiy f paneedyel'neek ee va ftorneek. Mashina p'yot beenzeen!

13 Gdye z'des' kheemcheestka? Oo meenya masla na foodbolkee 'Armanee'.

14 Nasha kvarteera za glavnaiy ooleetseiy, oo (or okala) astanofkee aftoboosa.

15 Mi v meeleetsi-ee, patamoo shta mi nee znaeem, gdye moiy sotaviy teeleefon.

16 Nada koopeet' beelyeti seechyas, patamoo shta anee deeshevlee.

17 Mnye nraveetsa vasha mashina. Ana ocheen' doraga stoeela?

18 Vi nee mozhitee nam pamoch'? Mozhna z'dyes' yes't' okala reekee?

WEEK 6

QUIZ

1b, 2c, 3d, 4a, 5d, 6b, 7c, 8b, 9a, 10b/d

SPOT THE KEYS

Depends when you travel. Usually 20 minutes, but at rush hour when traffic jams everywhere, journey might last 45 minutes. Cost usually between 30 and 50 roubles.

SAY IT SIMPLY

1 Eezveeneetee, pazhaloosta, ya v nomeere 222. Tam teeleeveezar nee rabotaeet ee doosh nee rabotaeet. Pazhaloosta, eekh nada atreemanteeravat'. Ya nadyeyus, shto vi mozhitee mnye pamoch'!

2 Zdrastvooiytee. Gavareet Kate Green. Ya bila v vasheiy gasteeneetse, v nomeeree... K sazhilyeneeyu ya oozhe v aerapartoo, a maya soomka v nomeeree. Pazhaloosta, mayu soomkoo nada v Angleeyu. Gasteeneetsa znaeet, gdye ya zhivoo. Spaseeba bal'shoye.

TEST YOUR PROGRESS

1 Mnye nraveetsa peesat' pees'ma, patamoo shta oo meenya noviiy kamp'yutir.
2 Kak deela? Oo vas prablyema? Vam pamoch'?
3 Eezveeneetee, oo vas yes't' nomeer yeeyo sotavava teeleefona?
4 Mnye nraveetsa Krim. Tam neekagda nee kholadna.
5 Droogoiy cheemadan v aftoboosee. Oo vas kareechneevaya soomka?
6 Gdye vi boodeetee na Razhdeestvo?
7 Kto khocheet riboo ee kto khocheet myasa?
8 Oo neevo moiy nomeer teeleefona. On chyasta zvaneet mnye.
9 Skaryeye! Gdye beelyet? Poeest eedyot!
10 Vi nee znaeete, shto aeraport vseegda atkrit?
11 Moiy otpoosk ocheen' vazhniy. Ya khachu v Italeeyu.
12 Vi veedeelee Ol'goo v gazyetee? Beez moozha?
13 Vasha mama ocheen' preeyatnaya. Yeeyo aryekhaviy tort ocheen' fkoosniy!
14 Nam nada rabotat'. Oo nas tree mal'cheeka ee adna dyevachka. Ocheen' doraga stoeet!
15 Eezveeneetee, gdye mozhna atreemanteeravat' mashinoo?
16 Mi yeevo znaeem. On vseegda dyelaeet pakoopkee s sabakaiy.
17 Kto skazal, shto z'dyes' neel'zya kooreet'?
18 Mi yedeem v aeraport na taksee, patom v Dallas na samalyotee.
19 Ya khachu gavareet' s afeetseeantam. Gdye shshyot?
20 Eezveeneetee, no eta kanyets **Fast-track Russian**.

....
YOUR SCORE: _____%
....

Russian–English dictionary

In this section you'll find all the **New words** that you have learned, including the 'extras', in alphabetical order. This is a quick guide to the complete **fast-track** vocabulary.

To make it easy for you to find what you may have forgotten, words are shown exactly as they appear in the **New words** section. For example, if you learned *a few* you'll find it under 'a'. If you don't remember how to say *I work* you'll find it under 'I'.

a   *and, but*
abratna   *back/return*
adeen   *one*
adeenatsat'   *eleven*
afeetsiant   *waiter*
aftoboos/aftoboosee   *bus*
aktyabr'   *October*
ana   *she*
angleeskaya/Angleeya,
  Anglee-ee   *English/England*
apryel'   *April*
aptyeka/aptyekoo   *chemist's*
aranzhiviiy   *orange*
aryekhaviy tort   *walnut cake*
astanofka   *bus stop*
atkhadeet'/atkhodeet   *to leave/
  it leaves*
atkooda   *from where*
atkriti   *open (plural form)*
atreemanteeravat'   *to repair*
atsyuda   *from here*
avgoost   *August*

bal'na   *ill, sick*
bal'neetsa/bal'neetsoo   *hospital*
bal'shaya   *big*
baleet   *it hurts*
bank/v bankee   *bank/in, at bank*
banka/bankoo   *tin, jar*
bar   *bar*
beefshteks   *steak*
beelyet/beelyety   *ticket/tickets*
beenzazaprafka   *petrol station
  (colloquial)*
beenzeen   *petrol*
bees teeleefona   *without telephone*
bil   *was*
bilee   *were*
bleeska   *close, near*
bol'shi   *more*
boodoo/boodeet   *I will be/he
  (she, it) will be*
boomaga/boomagee   *paper*
bootilkoo shampanskava   *bottle
  of champagne*

bootirbr**o**t/bootirbr**o**di *sandwich/sandwiches*

B**o**zhe moiy! *Good grief! (lit: God my!)*

br**o**shka/br**o**shkoo *brooch*

b**ye**liiy *white*

cheelav**ye**k *person*

cheemad**a**n/cheemad**a**nam *suitcase*

chees**i** *clock*

ch**ee**stiee *clean*

cheet**i**ree *four*

cheet**i**reesta *four hundred*

cheet**i**rnatsat' *fourteen*

cheet**vye**rk *Thursday*

chyaiy *tea*

chyas *hour*

chy**a**sta *often*

chy**o**rniiy *black*

da *yes*

da kak**o**va chy**a**sa? *until when?*

da sveed**a**neeya *goodbye*

d**a**chya *summer house*

d**aiy**tee *give!*

d**ee**kabr' *December*

deesh**ye**vlee *cheaper*

deeveen**o**sta *ninety*

deeveetn**a**tsat' *nineteen*

dlya *for*

dlya meen**ya** *for me*

dny**eiy**/dny**a** *days*

do, da *until*

d**o**braye **oo**tra *good morning*

d**o**briiy dyen' *good day, good afternoon*

d**o**briiy v**ye**cheer *good evening*

doch *daughter*

dom *house*

d**oo**mat'/d**oo**mayu *to think/ I think*

doosh (z d**oo**shim) *shower (with a shower)*

d**o**raga *expensive*

droog/dr**oo**goo *friend*

droog**oiy** *other, another*

dva *two*

dva beel**ye**ta *two tickets*

dv**a**tsat' *twenty*

dveen**a**tsat' *twelve*

dvye *(f.) two*

dv**ye**r/dv**ee**ree *door*

dv**ye**s'tee *two hundred*

d**ye**la *matter*

d**ye**lat' *to do*

dyen' *day*

d**ye**neek *money*

d**ye**seet' *ten*

d**ye**tee *children*

d**ye**vachka/d**ye**vachkee *(little) girl/girls*

d**ye**veet'/deeveet**ee** *nine*

ee *and*

eed**yo**t *(he, she) it goes, is going*

eed**yo**t dosht' *it's raining*

eekr**a**/eekri *caviar*

eelee *or*

eem *to them*

eenteer**ye**sna *it is interesting*

eeyul' *July*
ee**yu**n' *June*
eez, ees *from*
eezveen**ee** *I am sorry (informal)*
eezveen**ee**tee *excuse me*
eta *it is*
etat/**e**ta *this*

f kat**o**ram chees**oo**? *at what time?*
f pyat chees**of** *at five o'clock*
f sl**ye**dooshshee/**e**tam gad**oo** *next/this year*
f syem' treetsat' *at 7.30*
f tree cheesa *at three o'clock*
fatagr**a**fiya/ fatagr**a**feeiy *photograph/ photographs*
f**ee**rma/f**ee**rmi *firm*
f**ee**rmeeniee bl**yu**da *firm's dishes (i.e. specials)*
feevr**a**l' *February*
foodb**o**lka *T-shirt*
fr**oo**kt *fruit*
fstr**ye**chya *meeting*
fsyo *all, everything*
ft**o**rneek/ft**o**rneeka *Tuesday*

gaspad**ee**n *Mr*
gaspazh**a** *Mrs*
gat**o**vi *ready*
Gav**ai**yee *Hawaii*
gavar**ee**t'/gavar**ee**t *to speak, to say/he speaks, he says*
gaz**ye**ta *newspaper*
gdye *where*
gl**a**vnaia **oo**leetsa *main street*
g**o**da/got *year*
g**o**rad, g**o**rat *town*

got *year*
gr**ee**l'/gr**ee**lya *grill*
iksk**oo**rseeya *excursion*
Ital**ee**ya/v **I**tal**ee**yu *Italy/to Italy*
k sazhil**ye**neeyu *unfortunately*
kaf**e** *café*
kagd**a** *when*
kak deel**a**? *how are things?*
kak pa-**roo**skee? *how in Russian?*
kak**oiy**-ta *some (sort of)*
kalbas**a**/kalbas**oo** *sausage*
kamp'**yu**tir/kamp'**yu**tiri *computer*
kan**ye**shna *of course*
kan**ye**ts *end, direction (one way)*
kar**ee**chneeviiy *brown*
k**a**zhitsa *it seems, I think/believe*
khal**o**dniy *cold*
kharash**o** *good, well*
khar**o**chaya *good*
kheemch**ee**stka/kheemch**ee**stkoo *dry cleaner's*
kh**o**ladna *cold*
klee**ye**nt *customer*
kn**ee**ga *book*
k**o**fee *coffee*
k**o**ncheelsa/k**o**ncheelas' *has finished*
koop**ee**la *I bought*
koop**ee**t'/koop**ee**la *to buy/she bought*
koor**ee**t' *to smoke*
k**oo**reetsa/k**oo**reetsi *chicken*
koos**o**cheek *piece*
kras**a**veets *handsome fellow*
kras**ee**viiy *beautiful*
kr**a**sniiy *red*

kreed**ee**tniee k**a**rtachkee   *credit cards*

kto   *who*

kto tak**oiy**… ?   *who is… ?*

kto-ta   *someone*

kvart**ee**ra   *flat*

L**a**da/L**a**doo   *Lada*

l**oo**chshe   *better*

lyet   *of years*

Mad**yeiy**ra/Mad**yeiy**roo   *Madeira*

magaz**ee**n/magaz**ee**nee   *shop/shops*

m**a**iy   *May*

m**a**l'cheek   *boy*

m**a**la   *few, little*

malak**o**/malak**o**m   *milk*

m**a**leen'keeiy/m**a**leen'k**a**ya   *small*

m**a**mi/m**a**ma   *mother*

m**a**rkee/m**a**rkamee   *stamps*

mart   *March*

mash**i**na   *car*

m**a**sla   *oil*

matr**yo**shka/matr**yo**shkee   *Russian doll/dolls*

ma**ya**, moiy   *my*

meel**ee**tsiya   *police*

meen**oo**ta   *minute*

meen**oo**tachkoo   *little minute*

meen**ya** zav**oo**t   *they call me (I am called)*

meen**yu**   *menu*

meest**a**   *places, seats*

mi   *we*

mi khat**ee**m   *we want*

mn**o**ga   *many*

moosh   *husband*

mooz**yeiy**/mooz**ye**ya   *museum*

m**o**zhit bit'   *perhaps*

m**o**zhna   *it is possible*

m**ya**sa   *meat*

m**ye**dleena   *slowly*

m**ye**seets   *month*

Myeseetsi   *months*

na   *for, on*

na adn**oo** noch   *for one night*

na cheelav**ye**ka   *for a person (per person)*

na des**ya**tam itazh**e**   *on the tenth floor*

n**a**da   *it is necessary*

nad**ye**yatsa/nad**ye**yus'   *to hope/ I hope*

nal**ye**va   *to the left, on the left*

nam   *for us*

napr**a**va   *to the right, on the right*

naveerkh**oo**   *upstairs*

na**ya**br'   *November*

nee dal**ee**ko   *it is (not) far, (not) distant*

nee gad**ee**tsa   *it does not fit (it's not on)*

nee rab**o**taeet   *does not work*

neech**ee**staya   *not clean*

neech**ee**vo   *nothing*

need**ye**lya   *week*

neekagd**a** nee   *never*

neekoor**ya**shshiye   *non-smokers*

neekt**o**   *no one*

neel'z**ya**   *it is not possible, one may not*

neemn**o**shka   *a little*

neeplakh**o**ye   *not bad*

no   *but*

n**o**meer   *number*
n**o**meer na dv**aee**kh   *room for two (i.e. double room)*
noo...   *well...*
n**o**viy/n**o**vim   *new*
nye   *not*
nye pr**a**vda lee   *isn't it?*
n**ye**skal'ka   *a few*
nyet   *no*
nyet prabl**ye**m!   *no problem!*

oba   *both*
ocheen'   *very*
okala   *near, by*
on   *it/he*
on/yev**o**/neem   *he, him*
oo meen**ya**   *I have*
oo nas   *by us (we have)*
oo nee**yo**   *she has*
ooneeveerm**a**g/ooneeveerm**a**gee   *department store*
oov**ee**deet'/oov**ee**deela   *to see/she saw*
oozh**a**snaya, oozh**a**sniiy   *terrible*
oozh**e**   *already*

pa b**ee**znisoo   *on business*
pa vaskrees**ye**neeyam   *on Sundays*
pachem**oo**   *why*
pacht**o**viy **ya**shsheek   *post box*
pad**a**rkee/pad**a**rkaf   *presents*
padazhd**ee**!   *wait!*
padr**oo**ga   *girlfriend*
pag**o**da   *weather*
pak**oo**pkee   *the shopping*
pak**ye**teek   *bag*
pam**o**ch'   *to help*

pam**ye**dleeneeye   *a little more slowly*
paneedy**el**'neek   *Monday*
par**a**   *it is time (to go)*
par**a**/par**oo**   *pair, couple*
pareekm**a**kheerskaya/ pareekm**a**kheer- skooyu   *hairdresser's*
patam**oo** shta   *because*
patkhad**ya**shsheeiy/ patkhad**ya**shsheeva   *suitable*
pat**o**m   *then, next*
pay**e**deem   *let's go*
pay**e**stka   *journey*
pazh**a**loosta   *please*
pazvan**ee**t'/pazvan**ee**l   *to ring/he rang*
peedees**ya**t   *fifty*
p**ee**s'ma   *letters*
pees'm**o**   *letter*
p**ee**shim   *we write*
peet'/ya p'yu   *to drink/I drink*
peetn**a**tsat'   *fifteen*
peets**o**t   *five hundred*
p**ee**va   *beer*
plakh**a**ya   *bad*
plan g**o**rada   *plan of the town*
platf**o**rma/platf**o**rmi   *platform*
po, pa   *on, along, according to*
p**o**chta/p**o**chtoo   *post office*
po**ee**st/f po**ee**zdee   *train/in the train*
p**o**lan   *full*
poot'/poot**ee**   *way, journey*
p**o**zna   *it is late*
pradav**ye**ts   *shop assistant*
pragram**ee**st   *computer programmer*

prakampast**ee**ravat' *to punch, clip*

prashl**o** *it went by, passed*

prast**oo**da *a cold*

preeglash**a**t'/preeglash**a**yu *to invite/I invite*

preekr**a**snaya *splendid*

preeneem**a**eem *we accept*

pree**ya**tniiy *pleasant*

pr**ya**ma *straight on*

pyat' *five*

p**ya**tneetsa *Friday*

p**ye**rvyiy *first*

rab**o**ta *work, job*

rab**o**taeetee *you work*

rab**o**tal *I, he worked*

rab**o**tala *I, she worked*

rab**o**tayu *I work*

rad**ee**teelee *parents*

Razhdeestv**o** *Christmas*

reek**a** *river*

r**i**ba/r**i**boo *fish*

roobl**ee**, roobl**yeiy** *rouble(s)*

r**o**zaviiy *pink*

s oom**a** sashl**a** *crazy! (to a man one would say:* s ooma s**a**shol)

s v**a**naiy *with a bathroom*

s vas'm**ee** cheesof *from eight hours (from eight o'clock)*

s, z *with, from*

sab**a**ka *dog*

s**a**khar/s**a**khara *sugar*

sal**a**t/sal**a**tam *salad*

samal**yo**t(ee) *aeroplane*

seech**ya**s *now*

seemn**a**tsat' *seventeen*

seeneey *blue*

seent**ya**br' *September*

seev**o**dnya *today*

shamp**a**nskaye *champagne*

sh**e**s't' *six*

shikal**a**t *chocolate*

shisn**a**tsat' *sixteen*

shis**o**t *six hundred*

shiz'dees**ya**t *sixty*

shk**o**la *school*

shsh**yo**t *bill*

sht**o** *what, that*

sin *son*

s**i**r/s**i**ram *cheese*

skar**ye**ye *hurry*

skaz**a**t'/skaz**a**l *to say/he said*

sk**o**l'ka *how much/how many*

sk**oo**chnaya *boring*

slam**a**las' *it has broken down*

sl**a**tkaye *sweet, dessert*

sl**ee**shkam *too (as in too much)*

sl**oo**shayu *I listen*

sl**ye**dooshshyeeiy *next*

smatr**ye**t' *to watch*

snach**ya**la *first*

snyat' *to take (of photographs)*

snyek/sneeg**oo** *snow*

s**o**ntse *sun*

soob**o**ta *Saturday*

s**oo**mka, s**oo**mkee *bag*

soop *soup*

soopeerm**a**rkeet *supermarket*

sooveen**ee**ri/ sooveen**ee**raf *souvenirs*

s**o**rak *forty*

s**o**taviy (teeleef**o**n) *mobile (telephone)*

spas**ee**ba/balsh**oiy**e *thank you/ very much*

sport/sp**o**rta/sp**o**rtoo *sport*

sreed**a** *Wednesday*

S-SHA *USA*

stak**a**n *glass*

st**a**ntseeya meetr**o** *metro station*

st**a**roye/st**a**raya *old*

sto *hundred*

st**o**eet *costs*

stol *table*

sveetaf**o**r/sveetaf**o**ra *traffic lights*

sv**o**dyat meen**ya** s oom**a** *are driving me crazy*

syem' *seven*

syem' s**o**rak pyat' *7.45*

s**ye**mdeesyat *seventy*

s**ye**riiy *grey*

tak *thus, so*

tak**oiy** zhe ... kak *just as ... as*

taks**ee** *taxi*

tam *there*

teeleev**ee**zar/ teeleev**ee**zaroo *television*

teeplakh**o**t/teeplakh**o**dee *ship*

t**e**nees *tennis*

tis**ee**chya *thousand*

t**o**l'ka *only*

tooal**ye**ti *toilets*

tood**a** *to there*

t**o**zhe *also*

tree *three*

tree chees**a** *it is three o'clock*

treen**a**tsat' *thirteen*

tr**ee**sta *three hundred*

tr**ee**tsat m**ye**traf *30 metres*

tr**ee**tsat' *thirty*

tsentr *centre*

ts**e**rkaf'/ts**e**rkav'yu *church*

Tsifri *numerals*

Tsv**ee**ta *colours*

t**yo**mnava m**ya**sa *dark (red) meat*

v **a**vgoos'tee *in August*

v dva chees**a** *at two o'clock*

v m**a**ee *in May*

v ooneev**ee**erseet**ye**tee *at a/the university*

v **o**tpooskee *on holiday*

v toorag**ye**ntstvee *in a/the travel agency*

v, va, f *in, to, at*

vad**a**/vad**i** *water*

vagz**a**l *(railway) station*

vapr**o**s *question*

vaseemn**a**tsat *eighteen*

vaskreesy**e**n'ye *Sunday*

v**a**zhniee *important*

vazm**o**zhna *it is possible*

veetcheen**a**/veetcheen**oiy** *ham*

v**ee**deet'/v**ee**zhoo *to see/I see*

veeleekal**ye**pna *splendid(ly), great, wonderful(ly)*

veen**o** *wine*

vi *you (polite)*

vi/vas *you*

v**i**khad/v**i**khada *exit*

v**i**zvat' *... to summon, call, send for*

vneez**oo** *downstairs*

von tam *over there*

v**o**seem' *eight*

voseem' peetnatsat'   at 8.15
voseemdeesyat   eighty
vot   here (there) is/are
vrach/vrachya   doctor
vryedna   it is harmful
vryemya   time
Vryemya   telling the time
vseegda   always

ya   I
yantarnaya   amber
yanvar'   January
yedeem   we go (travel)
yedoo   I go (travel)
yelee   we/they ate
yes't'   there is/is there
yuveleerniy   jewellery

z'dyes'   here
za   for, behind, beyond
zaftra   tomorrow
zaftrak   breakfast
zaftrakat'   to have breakfast
zapreeshshaeetsa   it is forbidden
zdrastvooiytee   hello
zeelyoniiy   green
zhareenaiy kartoshkaiy   fried potato
zhdat'   to wait
zhina   wife
zhirna   it is greasy
zhivyot   lives
zholtiiy   yellow
znat'/znayu/znaeet   to know/
  I know/he/(she) knows
zvaneet   rings, phones

English–Russian dictionary

a few **ny**e**skal'ka**
a little neemn**o**shka
a little more slowly pam**y**ed-
  le-en**ee**ye
according to po, pa
aeroplane samal**yot**(ee)
all fsyo
along po, pa
already **oozhe**
also **tozhe**
always vseegd**a**
amber yant**a**rnaya
and a/ee
another droog**oiy**
April apr**yel'**
are driving me crazy sv**o**dyat
  meen**ya** s **oo**m**a**
at f
at a/the university
  v ooneev**ee**rseet**ye**tee
at five o'clock f pyat chees**of**
at seven thirty f syem' tr**ee**t sat'
at three o'clock f tree chees**a**
at two o'clock v dva chees**a**
at what time? f kat**o**ram
  chees**oo**?
August **a**vgoost

back abr**a**tna
bad plakh**a**ya
bag pak**ye**teek,
  s**oo**mka, s**oo**mkee
bank/in, at bank bank/v
  b**a**nkee

bar bar
beautiful kras**ee**viiy
because patam**oo** shta
beer **pee**va
behind za
better l**oo**chshe
beyond za
big bal'sh**a**ya
bill shsh**yo**t
black ch**yo**rniiy
blue s**ee**neey
book kn**ee**ga
boring sk**oo**chnaya
both **o**ba
bottle of champagne boot**i**lka
  shamp**a**nskava
boy m**a**l'cheek
breakfast z**a**ftrak
brooch br**o**shka/br**o**shkoo
brown kar**ee**chneeviiy
bus aft**o**boos/aft**o**boosee
bus stop astan**o**fka
but a, no
by **o**kala
by us (we have) oo nas

café kaf**e**
call vizv**a**t'…
car m**a**shina
caviar eekr**a**/eekr**i**
centre tsentr
champagne shamp**a**nskaye
cheaper deesh**ye**vlee
cheese sir/sir**a**m

chemist's   ap**tye**ka/ap**tye**koo
chicken   **koo**reetsa/**koo**reetsi
children   **dye**tee
chocolate   shika**lat**
Christmas   Razhdeestvo
church   ts**er**kaf'/ts**er**kav'yu
clean   **chee**stiee
clip   prakampas**tee**ravat'
clock   **chee**si
close   bl**ee**ska
coffee   **ko**fee
cold   prast**oo**da, khal**o**dniy/
   khol**a**dna
colours   tsv**ee**ta
computer   kamp'**yu**tir/
   kamp'**yu**tiri
computer programmer
   pragram**ee**st
costs   st**o**eet
couple   **pa**roo
crazy!   s oo**ma** sash**la** (to a man
   one would say: s oo**ma** sas**hol**)
credit cards   kreed**ee**tniee
   kartachkee
customer   klee**ye**nt

dark (red) meat   **tyo**mnava
   myasa
daughter   doch
day   dyen'
days   dn**yeiy**/dn**ya**
December   d**ee**kabr'
department store   oonee**veer**mag/
   oonee**veer**magee
dessert   sl**a**tkaye
direction (one way)   kan**ye**ts
doctor   vrach/vrach**ya**
does not work   nee rab**o**taeet

dog   sab**a**ka
door   dv**yer**/dv**er**ee
downstairs   vnee**zoo**
dry cleaner's   kheemch**ee**stka/
   kheemch**ee**stkoo

eight   **vo**seem'
eight fifteen   **vo**seem'
   peetn**a**tsat
eighteen   vas**ee**mnatsat
eighty   **vo**seemdeesyat
eleven   ad**ee**natsat'
end, direction (one way)   kan**ye**ts
England   **A**ngleeya, **A**nglee-ee
English   angl**ee**skaya
everything   fsyo
excursion   iksk**oo**rseeya
excuse me   eezv**ee**neetee
exit   vikhad/vikhada
expensive   d**o**raga

February   feevr**al**'
few   **ma**la
fifteen   peetn**a**tsat'
fifty   peedees**ya**t
firm   f**eer**ma/f**eer**mi
firm's dishes (i.e. specials)   f**eer**-
   meeniee bl**yu**da
first   sn**a**chyala, p**yer**vyiy
fish   r**i**ba/r**i**boo
five   pyat'
five hundred   peets**o**t
flat   kvart**ee**ra
for   na, za, dlya
for a person (per person)   na
   cheelav**ye**ka
for me   dlya meen**ya**
for one night   na adn**oo** noch

for us   n**a**m
forty   s**o**rak
four   ch**ee**tiree
four hundred   ch**ee**tireesta
fourteen   ch**ee**t**i**rnatsat'
Friday   py**a**tneetsa
fried potato   zh**a**reenaiy
   kart**o**shkaiy
friend   dr**oo**g/dr**oo**goo
from   z, **ee**z, **ee**s
from eight hours (from eight
   o'clock)   s vas'm**ee** ch**ee**sof
from here   ats**yu**da
from where   atk**oo**da
fruit   fr**oo**kt
full   p**o**lan

girl/girls (little)   d**y**ev**a**chka/
   d**y**ev**a**chkee
girlfriend   padr**oo**ga
give!   d**a**iytee
glass   stak**a**n
good   khar**a**sho/khar**o**chaya
good afternoon   d**o**briiy dyen'
good day   d**o**briiy dyen'
good evening   d**o**briiy v**y**echeer
Good grief! (lit: God my!)   B**o**zhe
   m**o**iy!
good morning   d**o**braye **oo**tra
goodbye   da sveed**a**neeya
great   veeleekal**y**epna
green   zeel**y**oniiy
grey   s**y**eriiy
grill   gr**ee**l'/gr**ee**lya

hairdresser's   pareekm**a**kheer-
   skaya/pareekmakheersk**oo**yu
ham   veetch**ee**na/veetcheen**o**iy

handsome fellow   kras**a**veets
has finished   k**o**ncheelsa/
   k**o**nch**ee**las'
Hawaii   Gav**a**iyee
he   **o**n
he goes   eed**y**ot
he rang   pazvan**ee**l
he said   skaz**a**l
he says   gavar**ee**t
he speaks   gavar**ee**t
he worked   rab**o**tal
he/she knows   zn**a**eet
hello   zdr**a**stvooiytee
here   z'dyes'
here is/are   vot
him   y**e**vo, n**ee**m
hospital   bal'n**ee**tsa/
   bal'n**ee**tsoo
hour   ch**ya**s
house   dom
how are things?   kak deel**a**?
how in Russian?   kak
   pa-r**oo**skee?
how many   sk**o**l'ka
how much   sk**o**l'ka
hundred   sto
hurry   skar**y**eye
husband   moosh

I   ya
I am sorry (informal)   eezve-
   enee
I believe   k**a**zhitsa
I bought   koop**ee**la
I drink   ya p'yu
I go (travel)   y**e**doo
I have   oo meen**ya**
I invite   preeglash**a**yu*

I know zn**a**yu
I listen sl**oo**shayu
I see v**ee**zhoo
I think d**oo**mayu, k**a**zhitsa
I will be/he (she, it) will be b**oo**
doo/b**oo**deet
I work rab**o**tayu
I worked rab**o**tala, rab**o**tal
ill bal'n**a**
important v**a**zhniee
in v, v**a**, f
in a/the travel agency v
toorag**y**entstvee
in August v **a**vgoos'tee
in May v m**a**ee
in the train f p**o**eezdee
is going eed**yo**t
is there yes't'
isn't it? nye pr**a**vda lee
it on
it does not fit (it's not on) nee
gad**ee**tsa
it goes eed**yo**t
it has broken down slam**a**las'
it hurts bal**ee**t
it is **e**ta
it is (not) far, (not) distant nee
dal**ee**ko
it is forbidden zapr**ee**shshaeetsa
it is greasy zh**i**rna
it is harmful vr**ye**dna
it is interesting eenteer**ye**sna
it is late p**o**zna
it is necessary n**a**da
it is not possible neel'z**ya**
it is possible vazm**o**zhna,
m**o**zhna
it is raining eed**yo**t dosht'

it is three o'clock tree ch**ee**s**a**
it is time (to go) par**a**
it leaves atkh**o**deet
it seems k**a**zhitsa
it went by prashl**o**
Italy/to Italy It**a**leeya/v
It**a**leeyu

January yanv**a**r'
jar b**a**nka/bank**oo**
jewellery yuvel**ee**rniy
job rab**o**ta
journey pa**ye**stka, poot**ee**,
poot'
July ee**yu**l'
June ee**yu**n'
just as… as tak**oi**y zhe… kak

Lada L**a**da/Lad**oo**
let's go pa**ye**deem
letter/letters pees'm**o**/p**ee**s'm**a**
little m**a**la
little minute meen**oo**tachkoo
lives zhiv**yo**t

Madeira Mad**ye**iyra/
Mad**ye**iyr**oo**
main street gl**a**vnaiy **oo**leetsi
many mn**o**ga
March mart
matter d**ye**la
May m**a**iy
meat m**ya**sa
meeting fstr**ye**chya
menu meen**yu**
metro station st**a**ntseeya
m**ee**tro
milk malak**o**/malak**o**m

minute **meenoota**
mobile (telephone) **sotaviy (teeleefon)**
Monday **paneedyel'neek**
money **dyeneek**
month/s **myeseets/Myeseetsi**
more **bol'shi**
mother **mami/mama**
Mr **gaspadeen**
Mrs **gaspazha**
museum **moozyeiy/moozyeya**
my **maya, moiy**

near **bleeska, okala**
never **neekagda nee**
new **noviy/novim**
newspaper **gazyeta**
next **patom, slyedooshshyeeiy**
next/this year **f slyedooshshee/etam gadoo**
nine **dyeveet'/deeveetee**
nineteen **deeveetnatsat'**
ninety **deeveenosta**
no **nyet**
no one **neekto**
no problem! **nyet prablyem!**
non-smokers **neekooryas-hshiye**
not **nye**
not bad **neeplakhoye**
not clean **neecheestaya**
nothing **neecheevo**
November **nayabr'**
now **seechyas**
number **nomeer**
numerals **tsifri**

October **aktyabr'**
of course **kanyeshna**

of years **lyet**
often **chyasta**
oil **masla**
old **staroye/staraya**
on **na, po, pa**
on business **pa beeznisoo**
on holiday **v otpooskee**
on Sundays **pa vaskreesye-neeyam**
on the left **nalyeva**
on the right **naprava**
on the tenth floor **na desyatam itazhe**
one **adeen**
one may not **neel'zya**
only **tol'ka**
open (plural form) **atkriti**
or **eelee**
orange **aranzhiviiy**
other **droogoiy**
over there **von tam**

pair **para**
paper **boomaga/boomagee**
parents **radeeteelee**
passed **prashlo**
perhaps **mozhit bit'**
person **cheelavyek**
petrol **beenzeen**
petrol station (colloquial) **been-zazaprafka**
phones **zvaneet**
photograph/photographs **fata-grafiya/fatagrafeeiy**
piece **koosocheek**
pink **rozaviiy**
places **meesta**
plan of the town **plan gorada**

platform   platforma/platformi
pleasant   preeyatniiy
please   pazhaloosta
police   meeleetsiya
post box   pachtoviy yashsheek
post office   pochta/pochtoo
presents   padarkee/padarkaf

question   vapros

ready   gatovi
red   krasniiy
return   abratna
rings   zvaneet
river   reeka
room for two (i.e. double
   room)   nomeer na dvaeekh
rouble(s)   rooblee, rooblyeiy
Russian doll/dolls   matryoshka/
   matryoshkee

salad   salat/salatam
sandwich/sandwiches   bootirbrot/
   bootirbrodi
Saturday   soobota
sausage   kalbasa/kalbasoo
school   shkola
seats   meesta
send for   vizvat'...
September   seentyabr'
seven   syem'
seven forty-five   syem' sorak
   pyat'
seventeen   seemnatsat'
seventy   syemdeesyat
she   ana
she bought   koopeela
she goes   eedyot

she has   oo neeyo
she knows   znaeet
she saw   ooveedeela
she worked   rabotala
ship   teeplakhot/teeplakhodee
shop assistant   pradavyets
shop/shops   magazeen/
   magazeenee
shopping, the shopping
   pakoopkee
shower (with a shower)   doosh
   (z dooshim)
sick   bal'na
six   shes't'
six hundred   shisot
sixteen   shisnatsat'
sixty   shiz'deesyat
slowly   myedleena
small   maleen'keeiy/
   maleen'kaya
snow   snyek/sneegoo
so   tak
some (sort of)   kakoiy-ta
someone   kto-ta
son   sin
soup   soop
souvenirs   sooveeneeri/
   sooveeneeraf
splendid   preekrasnaya
splendidly   veeleekalyepna
sport   sport/sporta/sportoo
stamps   markee/markamee
station (railway)   vagzal
steak   beefshteks
straight on   pryama
sugar   sakhar/sakhara
suitable   patkhadyashsheeiy/
   patkhadyashsheeva

suitcase cheemad**a**n/
  cheemad**a**nam
summer house **d**achya
sun **s**ontse
Sunday vaskreesyen'ye
supermarket soopeerm**a**rkeet
sweet sl**a**tkaye

table stol
taxi taks**ee**
tea chy**a**iy
television teeleev**ee**zar/
  teeleev**ee**zaroo
telling the time skaz**a**t vry**e**mya
ten d**ye**seet'
tennis t**e**nees
terrible oozh**a**snaya, oozh**a**sniiy
thank you/very much spas**ee**ba/
  balsh**oi**ye
that shto
then pat**o**m
there tam
there is y**e**s't'
there is/are vot
they ate y**e**lee
*they call me (I am
  called)* me**e**n**ya** zav**oo**t
thirteen treen**a**tsat'
thirty tr**e**etsat'
thirty metres tr**e**etsat m**ye**traf
this **e**tat/**e**ta
thousand tis**ee**chya
three tree
three hundred tre**e**sta
Thursday cheetv**ye**rk
thus tak
ticket/tickets beel**ye**t/beel**ye**ty
time vry**e**mya

tin b**a**nka/b**a**nkoo
to va
to buy koop**ee**t'
to do d**ye**lat'
to drink peet'
to have breakfast z**a**ftrakat'
to help pam**o**ch'
to hope/I hope nad**ye**yatsa/
  nad**ye**yus'
to invite preeglash**a**t'
to know znat'/zn**a**yu/zn**a**eet
to leave atkh**a**deet'
to punch prakampast**ee**ravat'
to repair atreemant**ee**ravat'
to ring pazvan**ee**t'
to say skaz**a**t'
to see oov**ee**deet', v**ee**deet'
to smoke koor**ee**t'
to speak gavar**ee**t'/gavar**ee**t
to summon v**i**zvat'…
to take (of photographs) snyat'
to the left nal**ye**va
to the right napr**a**va
to them eem
to there tood**a**
to think d**oo**mat'
to wait zhdat'
to watch smatr**ye**t'
today seev**o**dnya
toilets t**oo**alyeti
tomorrow z**a**ftra
too (as in too much) sl**ee**shkam
town g**o**rad, g**o**rat
traffic lights sveetaf**o**r/
  sveetaf**o**ra
train po**e**est
T-shirt foodb**o**lka
Tuesday ft**o**rneek/ft**o**rneeka

twelve   dveenatsat'
twenty   dvatsat'
two   dva, dvye (f)
two hundred   dvyes'tee
two tickets   dva beelyeta

unfortunately   k sazhilyeneeyu
until   do, da
until when?   da kakova
  chyasa?
upstairs   naveerkhoo
USA   S-SHA

very   ocheen'

wait!   padazhdee!
waiter   afeetsiant
walnut   cake aryekhaviy tort
was   bil
water   vada/vadi
way   poot'
we   mi
we accept   preeneemaeem
we   ate yelee
we go (travel)   yedeem
we want   mi khateem
we write   peeshim

weather   pagoda
Wednesday   sreeda
week   needyelya
well   kharasho
well   ... noo...
were   bilee
what   shto
when   kagda
where   gdye
white   byeliiy
who   kto
who is... ?   kto takoiy... ?
why   pachemoo
wife   zhina
wine   veeno
with   s
with a bathroom   s vanaiy
without telephone   bees
  teeleefona
wonderful(ly)   veeleekalyepna
work   rabota

year   goda/got
yellow   zholtiiy
yes   da
you (polite)/you   vi/vas
you work   rabotaeetee

Flash cards

The **Flash cards** have been voted the best part of this course!
Learning words and sentences can be tedious, but with flash cards
it's quick and good fun.

This is what you do:

When the **Day-by-day guide** tells you to use the cards, cut them
out. There are 22 **Flash words** and 10 **Flash sentences** for each
week. Each card has a little number on it telling you to which
week it belongs, so you won't cut out too many cards at a time or
muddle them up later on.

First, try to learn the words and sentences by looking at both sides of
the cards. Then, when you have a rough idea, start testing yourself.
That's the fun bit. Look at the English, say the Russian, and then
check. Make a pile each for the 'correct', 'wrong' and 'don't know'
ones. When all the cards are used up, start again with the 'wrong'
pile and try to whittle it down until you get all of them right. You
can also play it 'backwards' by starting with the Russian face-up.

Keep the cards in a little box or put an elastic band around them.
Take them with you on the bus, the train, to the hairdresser's or
the dentist's. If you find the paper too flimsy, photocopy the words
and sentences onto card before cutting them up. You could also
buy some plain card and stick them on or simply copy them out.

The 22 **Flash words** for each week are there to start you off. Convert
the rest of the **New words** to **Flash words,** too. It's well worth it!

FLASH CARDS for FAST-TRACK LEARNING:

DON'T LOSE THEM – USE THEM!

---

eezvee-neetee **1**	pazhaloosta **1**
oo nas **1**	da **1**
mi **1**	nyet **1**
ya **1**	yedoo **1**
vi **1**	rabotayu **1**
gdye **1**	rabota **1**

CUT OUT AND USE ✂

please **1**	excuse me **1**
yes **1**	by us (we have) **1**
no **1**	we **1**
I go (travel) **1**	I **1**
I work **1**	you **1**
work, job **1**	where **1**

CUT OUT AND USE ✂

128

kharoshiy/ kharoshaya [1]	dyeneek [1]
oo meenya [1]	eta [1]
bank, банк [1]	v otpooskee [1]
dom [1]	vseegda [1]
gorat [1]	sotaviy teeleefon [1]
nada [2]	skol'ka [2]

CUT OUT AND USE ✂

money [1]	good [1]
it is [1]	I have [1]
on holiday [1]	bank [1]
always [1]	house [1]
mobile phone [1]	town [1]
how much/ how many [2]	it is necessary [2]

CUT OUT AND USE ✂

rooblyeiy ²	na cheelavyeka ²
kreedeetniee kartachkee ²	zaftrak ²
mi khateem ²	mozhna ²
chyaiy ²	z'dyes' ²
bleeska ²	naprava ²
vi, vas ²	fsyo ²

CUT OUT AND USE ✂

2 per person	2 roubles
2 breakfast	2 credit cards
2 it is possible	2 we want
2 here	2 tea
2 on the right	2 near
2 all, everything	2 you

CUT OUT AND USE

oozhasniiy **2**	maleen'keeiy **2**
tooalyeti, M (gents), Ж (ladies) **2**	shshyot **2**
zaftra **2**	pryama **2**
stol **2**	mnoga **2**
na **3**	aftoboos(ee) **3**
plakhaya **3**	pochta/ pochtoo, почта **3**

CUT OUT AND USE ✂

small ²	terrible ²
bill ²	toilets ²
straight on ²	tomorrow ²
much, many ²	table ²
bus ³	on, by ³
post office ³	bad ³

CUT OUT AND USE ✂

markee 3	**neel'zya** 3
soomka 3	**ooneeveer- mag** 3
magazeen/ ee 3	**atkrit(i)** 3
nyet prablyem 3	**koopeet'** 3
shto 3	**neemnoshka** 3
gazyeta 3	**vot** 3

CUT OUT AND USE ✂

it's not possible	3	stamps	3
department store	3	bag	3
open	3	shop/s	3
to buy	3	no problem!	3
a little	3	what/that	3
here is, here are	3	newspaper	3

CUT OUT AND USE ✂

eedyot 3	**pagoda** 3
pakoopkee 3	**padarkee** 3
preekrasnaya 3	**kholadna** 3
kto-ta 4	**pachemoo** 4
nomeer 4	**kleeyent** 4
kharasho 4	**vazhniee** 4

CUT OUT AND USE ✂

weather [3]	(he, she, it) goes [3]
presents [3]	shopping [3]
cold [3]	splendid [3]
why [4]	someone [4]
client [4]	number [4]
important [4]	good, well [4]

CUT OUT AND USE ✂

kanyeshna <div align="right">4</div>	**eenteeryesna** <div align="right">4</div>
kagda <div align="right">4</div>	**spaseeba balshoie** <div align="right">4</div>
prastooda <div align="right">4</div>	**vrach/ vrachya** <div align="right">4</div>
riba/riboo <div align="right">4</div>	**beefshteks** <div align="right">4</div>
peeva <div align="right">4</div>	**stakan** <div align="right">4</div>
vada/vadi <div align="right">4</div>	**neekto** <div align="right">4</div>

CUT OUT AND USE ✂

it is interesting 4	of course 4
thank you very much 4	when 4
doctor 4	cold 4
steak 4	fish 4
glass 4	beer 4
no one 4	water 4

CUT OUT AND USE ✂

140

naveerkhoo 4	**okala** 4
kooreetsa 4	**pozna** 4
vagzal, вокзал 5	**abratna** 5
poeest 5	**zapree-shshaeetsa** 5
mala 5	**pees'mo** 5
pachtoviy yashsheek 5	**oba** 5

CUT OUT AND USE ✂

near, by 4	upstairs 4
it is late 4	chicken 4
back/return 5	(railway) station 5
it is forbidden 5	train 5
letter 5	few, little 5
both 5	post box 5

CUT OUT AND USE ✂

5 **pyervyiy**	5 **polan**
5 **droogoiy**	5 **etat/eta**
5 **mashina**	5 **staroye/ staraya**
5 **astanofka aftoboosa, остановка**	5 **glavnaiya ooleetsa**
5 **myedleena**	5 **meeleetsiya**
5 **skaryeye!**	5 **eedyot dosht'**

CUT OUT AND USE ✂

full	first
5	5

this	other, another
5	5

old	car
5	5

main street	bus stop
5	5

police	slowly
5	5

it's raining	hurry!
5	5

CUT OUT AND USE ✂

5 **shkola**	5 **bal'neetsa**
6 **Razhdeestvo**	6 **snyek/ sneegoo**
6 **payedeem**	6 **teeplakhot**
6 **S-SHA**	6 **veeleekal- yepna**
6 **chyasta**	6 **vneezoo**
6 **aeraport, аэропорт**	6 **neecheevo**

CUT OUT AND USE ✄

hospital 5	**school** 5
snow 6	**Christmas** 6
ship 6	**let's go** 6
great, wonderful 6	**USA** 6
downstairs 6	**often** 6
nothing 6	**airport** 6

CUT OUT AND USE ✂

6 **dyetee**	6 **mal'cheek**
6 **dyevachka**	6 **kneega**
6 **neekagda nee**	6 **radeeteelee**
6 **droog/ droogoo**	6 **para**
6 **kak deela?**	6 **padazhdee!**
6 **slyedoosh- shee**	6 **moosh**

CUT OUT AND USE ✂

boy	**children**
book	**(little) girl**
parents	**never**
it's time (to go)	**friend**
wait!	**how's things?**
husband	**next**

CUT OUT AND USE ✂

Meenya zavoot John. 1

Ya bil v Novgaradee. 1

pa beeznisoo 1

Oo meenya kvarteera. 1

Ya rabotayu v Londanee. 1

Oo nas sin ee doch. 1

Gdye vi rabotaeetee? 1

Mi yedeem v Maskvoo. 1

Rabota kharoshaya. 1

Vi v otpooskee? 1

CUT OUT AND USE ✂

My name is John. 1

I was in Novgorod. 1

on business 1

I have a flat. 1

I work in London. 1

We have a son and a daughter. 1

Where do you work? 1

We are going to Moscow. 1

The work is good. 1

Are you on holiday? 1

CUT OUT AND USE ✂

Oo vas yes't' nomeer? 2

On nye rabotaeet. 2

Skol'ka stoeet? 2

S vasmee da deeveetee. 2

Eta sleeshkam doraga! 2

Mi khateem v Novgarat. 2

Mi khateem bootirbrodi. 2

Z'dyes' yes't'...? 2

Gdye kafe? 2

F katoram cheesoo? 2

CUT OUT AND USE ✂

Do you have a room? 2

He isn't working. 2

How much is it? 2

From eight until nine. 2

This/It is too expensive! 2

We want to go to Novgorod. 2

We want some sandwiches. 2

Here there is...? 2

Where is the café? 2

At what time? 2

CUT OUT AND USE ✂

Seevodnya nam nada
dyelat' pakoopkee. 3

Gdye z'dyes' aftoboos? 3

Golf neel'zya smatryet'. 3

Nam nada v bank. 3

Ya khachu koopeet'
foodbolkoo. 3

Eta fsyo. 3

Gde z'dyes' magazeen
sooveeneeraf? 3

Magazeeni atkriti da
kakova chyasa? 3

Mi mnoga koopeelee. 3

Ocheen' doraga stoeet. 3

CUT OUT AND USE ✂

Today we must do/ go shopping	3
Is there a bus here?	3
It is not possible to watch golf.	3
It is necessary for us (to go) to a bank.	3
I want to buy a T-shirt.	3
That/It is all.	3
Where is there a souvenir shop?	3
Shops are open until what time?	3
We have bought a lot.	3
It is very expensive.	3

CUT OUT AND USE ✂

Kto-ta pazvaneel. 4

On nye skazal, pachemoo. 4

Oo meenya fstryechya s neem. 4

Ya yeevo znayu. 4

Tak neel'zya. 4

Shto vi khateetye peet'? 4

Shto vam? 4

Ocheen' vazhniee deela. 4

Vi nye mozhitee mnye pamoch'? 4

Kak pa-rooskee...? 4

CUT OUT AND USE ✂

Someone rang. 4

He didn't say why. 4

I have a meeting with him. 4

I know him. 4

One can't do that. 4

What do you want to drink? 4

What would you like? 4

A very important matter. 4

You couldn't help me, could you? 4

How do you say… in Russian? 4

CUT OUT AND USE

Gdye vagzal? 5

Kagda atkhodeet poeest? 5

Z'dyes' kooreet' zapreeshshaeetsa. 5

Da moozyeya daleeko? 5

Z'dyes' yes't' balneetsa? 5

Beelyetee nada prakampasteeravat'. 5

Mnye nye nraveetsa... 5

Taksee nee doraga stoeet, patamoo shta staroye. 5

Gdye maya soomka? 5

Ya nadyeyus', shto prablyem nye boodeet. 5

Where is the station? 5

When does the train leave? 5

It is forbidden to smoke here. 5

Is it far to the museum? 5

Is there a hospital here? 5

It is necessary to punch (clip) tickets. 5

I don't like... 5

The taxi is not expensive, because it is old. 5

Where is my bag? 5

I hope that there won't be any problems. 5

CUT OUT AND USE ✂

F paneedyelneek mnye nada boodeet rabotat'. 6

Ya nee magoo zhdat'. 6

Gdye vi zhivyotee? 6

Mnye nada koopeet' sotaviiy teeleefon. 6

Oo nas maleen'kaya kvarteera. 6

Oozhe kanyets nasheeva otpooska. 6

Z'dyes' neecheevo patkhadyashsheeva nyet. 6

V etam gadoo... 6

Kak deela? 6

Daiytee, pazhaloosta, gazyetoo. 6

CUT OUT AND USE ✂

On Monday I must work. 6

I can't wait. 6

Where do you live? 6

I must buy a mobile telephone. 6

We have a small flat. 6

Already it is the end of our holiday. 6

There's nothing suitable here. 6

This year... 6

How are you? 6

Please give me the/a newspaper. 6

CUT OUT AND USE ✂

This is to certify
that

....

has successfully completed
a six-week course of

Fast-track Russian

with

....
results

Date   *Author*

CONTINUE YOUR RUSSIAN STUDIES WITH OTHER TITLES FROM TEACH YOURSELF

Speak Russian with Confidence (takes you from Beginner to Level 2)		Rachel Farmer
3 audio CDs + booklet	ISBN: 978 144 410332 8	£17.99
Get Started in Russian (takes you from Beginner to Level 3)		Rachel Farmer
Book	ISBN: 978 144 410166 9	£9.99
Book/CD Pack	ISBN: 978 144 410167 6	£22.99
Audio support on 2 CDs	ISBN: 978 144 410168 3	£14.99
Complete Russian (takes you from Beginner to Level 4)		Daphne West
Book	ISBN: 978 144 410764 7	£14.99
Book/CD Pack	ISBN: 978 144 410765 4	£29.99
Audio support on 2 CDs	ISBN: 978 144 410766 1	£15.99
Learn to write Russian script		Daphne West
	ISBN: 978 144 410392 2	£6.99
Essential Russian Grammar		Daphne West
	ISBN: 978 144 410407 3	£6.99

WHY NOT LEARN ANOTHER LANGUAGE WITH ELISABETH SMITH?

THE FAST-TRACK *RANGE (TAKES YOU FROM BEGINNER TO LEVEL 2)*

Elisabeth Smith's Fast-track Spanish
Book	ISBN: 978 144 410030 3	£7.99
Book/CD Pack	ISBN: 978 144 410031 0	£17.99
Audio support on 2 CDs	ISBN: 978 144 410032 7	£14.99

Elisabeth Smith's Fast-track German
Book	ISBN: 978 144 410036 5	£7.99
Book/CD Pack	ISBN: 978 144 410037 2	£17.99
Audio support on 2 CDs	ISBN: 978 144 410038 9	£14.99

Elisabeth Smith's Fast-track French
Book	ISBN: 978 144 410033 4	£7.99
Book/CD Pack	ISBN: 978 144 410034 1	£17.99
Audio support on 2 CDs	ISBN: 978 144 410035 8	£14.99

Elisabeth Smith's Fast-track Italian
Book	ISBN: 978 144 410039 6	£7.99
Book/CD Pack	ISBN: 978 144 410040 2	£17.99
Audio support on 2 CDs	ISBN: 978 144 410041 9	£14.99

Elisabeth Smith's Fast-track Greek
Book	ISBN: 978 144 410042 6	£7.99
Book/CD Pack	ISBN: 978 144 410043 3	£17.99
Audio support on 2 CDs	ISBN: 978 144 410044 0	£14.99

Elisabeth Smith's Fast-track Portuguese
Book	ISBN: 978 144 410045 7	£7.99
Book/CD Pack	ISBN: 978 144 410046 4	£17.99
Audio support on 2 CDs	ISBN: 978 144 410047 1	£14.99

Elisabeth Smith's Fast-track Japanese
Book	ISBN: 978 144 410122 5	£7.99
Book/CD Pack	ISBN: 978 144 410123 2	£17.99
Audio support on 2 CDs	ISBN: 978 144 410124 9	£14.99

WHY NOT LEARN ANOTHER LANGUAGE WITH TEACH YOURSELF?

THE GET STARTED *RANGE (TAKES YOU FROM BEGINNER TO LEVEL 3)*

Get Started in Spanish — Mark Stacey and Angela González Hevia

Book	ISBN: 978 144 410067 9	£9.99
Book/CD Pack	ISBN: 978 144 410068 6	£22.99
Audio support on 2 CDs	ISBN: 978 144 410069 3	£14.99

Get Started in German — Rosi McNab

Book	ISBN: 978 144 410073 0	£9.99
Book/CD Pack	ISBN: 978 144 410074 7	£22.99
Audio support on 2 CDs	ISBN: 978 144 410075 4	£14.99

Get Started in French — Catrine Carpenter

Book	ISBN: 978 144 410070 9	£9.99
Book/CD Pack	ISBN: 978 144 410071 6	£22.99
Audio support on 2 CDs	ISBN: 978 144 410072 3	£14.99

Get Started in Italian — Vittoria Bowles

Book	ISBN: 978 144 410076 1	£9.99
Book/CD Pack	ISBN: 978 144 410077 8	£22.99
Audio support on 2 CDs	ISBN: 978 144 410078 5	£14.99

Get Started in Greek — Aristarhos Matsukas

Book	ISBN: 978 144 410161 4	£9.99
Book/CD Pack	ISBN: 978 144 410162 1	£22.99
Audio support on 2 CDs	ISBN: 978 144 410154 6	£14.99

Get Started in Japanese — Helen Gilhooly

Book	ISBN: 978 144 410155 3	£9.99
Book/CD Pack	ISBN: 978 144 410156 0	£22.99
Audio support on 2 CDs	ISBN: 978 144 410157 7	£14.99

Get Started in Hindi — Rupert Snell

Book	ISBN: 978 144 410158 4	£9.99
Book/CD Pack	ISBN: 978 144 410159 1	£22.99
Audio support on 2 CDs	ISBN: 978 144 410160 7	£14.99

Get Started in Portuguese   Sue Tyson-Ward
  Book   ISBN: 978 144 410552 0   £9.99
  Book/CD Pack   ISBN: 978 144 410553 7   £22.99
  Audio support on 2 CDs ISBN: 978 144 410554 4   £14.99

Get Started in Latin   G D A Sharpley
  Book   ISBN: 978 144 410163 8   £9.99
  Book/CD Pack   ISBN: 978 144 410164 5   £22.99
  Audio support on 2 CDs ISBN: 978 144 410165 2   £14.99

Get Started in Mandarin Chinese   Elizabeth Scurfield
                                                                 and Song Lianyi
  Book   ISBN: 978 144 410345 8   £9.99
  Book/CD Pack   ISBN: 978 144 410346 5   £22.99
  Audio support on 2 CDs ISBN: 978 144 410344 1   £14.99

Get Started in Turkish   Asuman Çelen
                                                                 Pollard
  Book   ISBN: 978 144 410549 0   £9.99
  Book/CD Pack   ISBN: 978 144 410550 6   £22.99
  Audio support on 2 CDs ISBN: 978 144 410551 3   £14.99

Get Started in Dutch   Gerdi Quist and
                                                                 Dennis Strik
  Book   ISBN: 978 144 410555 1   £9.99
  Book/CD Pack   ISBN: 978 144 410556 8   £22.99
  Audio support on 2 CDs ISBN: 978 144 410557 5   £14.99

Get Started in Polish   Joanna Michalak-Gray
  Book   ISBN: 978 144 410703 6   £9.99
  Book/CD Pack   ISBN: 978 144 410704 3   £22.99
  Audio support on 2 CDs ISBN: 978 144 410705 0   £14.99

Get Started in British Sign   Paul Redfern and
Language (BSL)   Deafworks
  Book/DVD Pack   ISBN: 978 034 099132 9   £19.99

A SELECTION FROM THE COMPLETE RANGE (TAKES YOU FROM BEGINNER TO LEVEL 4)

Complete Spanish   Juan Kattán-Ibarra
Book   ISBN: 978 144 410000 6   £12.99
Book/CD Pack   ISBN: 978 144 410001 3   £24.99
Audio support on 2 CDs   ISBN: 978 144 410002 0   £14.99

Complete German   Paul Coggle and
                                                           Heiner Schenke
Book   ISBN: 978 144 410008 2   £12.99
Book/CD Pack   ISBN: 978 144 410009 9   £24.99
Audio support on 2 CDs   ISBN: 978 144 410010 5   £14.99

Complete French   Gaëlle Graham
Book   ISBN: 978 144 410004 4   £12.99
Book/CD Pack   ISBN: 978 144 410005 1   £24.99
Audio support on 2 CDs   ISBN: 978 144 410006 8   £14.99

Complete Italian   Lydia Vellaccio and
                                                           Maurice Elston
Book   ISBN: 978 144 410012 9   £12.99
Book/CD Pack   ISBN: 978 144 410013 6   £24.99
Audio support on 2 CDs   ISBN: 978 144 410014 3   £14.99

Complete Greek   Aristarhos Matsukas
Book   ISBN: 978 144 410761 6   £14.99
Book/CD Pack   ISBN: 978 144 410762 3   £29.99
Audio support on 2 CDs   ISBN: 978 144 410763 0   £15.99

Complete Japanese   Helen Gilhooly
Book   ISBN: 978 144 410394 6   £15.99
Book/CD Pack   ISBN: 978 144 410395 3   £29.99
Audio support on 2 CDs   ISBN: 978 144 410396 0   £15.99

Complete Hindi   Rupert Snell and
                                                           Simon Weightman
Book   ISBN: 978 144 410609 1   £15.99
Book/CD Pack   ISBN: 978 144 410683 1   £29.99
Audio support on 2 CDs   ISBN: 978 144 410693 0   £15.99

Complete Portuguese		Manuela Cook
(takes you from Beginner		
to Level 4)		
Book	ISBN: 978 144 410767 8	£14.99
Book/CD Pack	ISBN: 978 144 410768 5	£29.99
Audio support on 2 CDs	ISBN: 978 144 410769 2	£15.99
Complete Latin		Gavin Betts
	ISBN: 978 144 410598 8	£17.99
Complete Mandarin Chinese		Elizabeth Scurfield
Book	ISBN: 978 034 095893 3	£15.99
Book/CD Pack	ISBN: 978 034 095894 0	£29.99
Audio support on 2 CDs	ISBN: 978 034 095895 7	£15.99
Complete Turkish		Sultan Erdoğan
		Smith
Book	ISBN: 978 144 410388 5	£14.99
Book/CD Pack	ISBN: 978 144 410239 0	£29.99
Audio support on 2 CDs	ISBN: 978 144 410248 2	£15.99
Complete Dutch		Gerdi Quist and
		Dennis Strik
Book	ISBN: 978 144 410599 5	£12.99
Book/CD Pack	ISBN: 978 144 410238 3	£24.99
Audio support on 2 CDs	ISBN: 978 144 410247 5	£14.99
Complete Polish		Nigel Gotteri and
		Joanna Michalak-Gray
Book	ISBN: 978 144 410608 4	£14.99
Book/CD Pack	ISBN: 978 144 410684 8	£29.99
Audio support on 2 CDs	ISBN: 978 144 410694 7	£15.99

For details of the full range of *Complete* titles, visit our website
www.teachyourself.com